Courageous Incarnation

In
Intimacy,
Work,
Childhood,
and
Aging

Fredrica Harris Thompsett

COWLEY PUBLICATIONS
Cambridge ✦ Boston
Massachusetts

Published in the United States of America by Cowley Publications, a division of the Society of St. John the Evangelist. No portion of this book may be reproduced, stored in or introduced into a retrieval system, or transmitted, in any form or by any means—including photocopying—without the prior written permission of Cowley Publications, except in the case of brief quotations embodied in critical articles and reviews.

International Standard Book Number: 1-56101-075-8
Library of Congress Number: 92-45781

All quotations are from the New Revised Standard Version of the Bible unless otherwise indicated.
"Some Children See Him," lyrics by Wihla Hutson and music by Alfred Burt, is used by permission of The Richmond Organization. (c) Copyright 1954 (renewed), 1957 (renewed), Hollis Music, Inc., New York, New York.

Library of Congress Cataloging-in-Publication Data
Thompsett, Fredrica Harris, 1942 -
    Courageous Incarnation : in intimacy, work, childhood, and aging / Fredrica Harris Thompsett.
      p. cm.
    Includes bibliographical references.
    ISBN 1-56101-075-8
    1. Sociology, Christian.   2. Church and social problems—Episcopal Church.   3. Incarnation.   4. Process theology.   5. Episcopal Church—Doctrines.   6. Anglican Communion—Doctrines.   I. Title.
    BX5930.2.T46   1993
    261.8—dc20   92-45781

Cowley Publications
28 Temple Place
Boston, Massachusetts 02111

For Robert George Harris
A father whose continuing wisdom,
like the doctrine of the
Incarnation, is a "rare cabinet
full of treasure."
(George Herbert)

Acknowledgments

This book comes literally from "talking out loud." As a church historian and contemporary theologian, I am blessed by seeking and finding wisdom not only in ancient scrolls but also among today's *laos tou theou*, the people of God. I am grateful to gracious hosts and challenging participants responding to early conference presentations of this material at the Province of New England Convocation (1988), the Kenyon Conference (1990), and the Finger Lakes Conference of Province II (1991).

Along the way friends and critics—and chief among these are recent students—have provoked my desire to articulate in contemporary terms what persons informed by Anglican incarnational theology believe and why. Current and former faculty colleagues of the Episcopal Divinity School—particularly John E. Booty, Carter Heyward, Suzanne R. Hiatt, Donald F. Winslow, and the late William J. Wolf—have informed these incarnational reflections. My teacher of economics, Noreen M. Carter, provided critical guidance and research assistance for chapters on work, childhood, and aging. As a teaching assistant, John L. Hooker touched my life with theological insight. The Conant Fund, administered by the Episcopal Board for Theological Education, provided funds to sustain a period of sabbatical study.

Offering abundant support and quieting good humor, my long-time friend Dorothy J. Brittain read early, middle, and late drafts of these chapters. In addition to Dorothy's inspiration, I have throughout this book drawn deeply from memories of relatives and close friends. These embodied witnesses, living and dead, have nurtured and informed my perceptions of God in Christ's incarnate presence amid the pressing challenges of these latter days. Through the graced fullness of such friendships, I am ever mindful of the spirited God who lives and loves among us.

Fredrica Harris Thompsett
Cambridge, Massachusetts

Table of Contents

1

Living Among Us

Incarnational Identity

I dentity messages are everywhere. In a variety of self-help books we are told: "Find yourself!" "Whatever your age, express who you really are!" "Be in touch with your true feelings." "Reclaim your lost sense of the child within." "Get your life together." How-to books advise individuals to "go for broke" in their workplaces and in their personal lives, seek new heights, rise above the daily grind. The methods of these voguish texts stress individual effort, often in isolation from other people, and their messages are a parody of incarnational living. God and our neighbors are seldom mentioned. We can observe an intemperate glorification of self in contemporary American culture: a pervasive identification of the individual as the defining core of life's meaning, a spirituality that seems to make a virtue if not of narcissism, at least of self-preoccupation. Many children and adults, influenced by television's invasive screen, have internalized these romantic images and unrealistic expectations of individual mastery over their lives. It is as if we believe we are truly separated, if not alone, in all creation.

Religious authorities are not immune from our culture's advocacy of searching for selfhood. With the commercialization of self-help in all branches of the media, it is no wonder religious leaders consciously and implicitly deliver similar messages. We are urged by some to "put God in our lives," or "to let Jesus into your life." I find such statements misleading at best, and at worst alarming; it had never occurred to me that I was not already part of God's creation, a child of God. God is in our lives whether we like it or not. The central biblical metaphor in both Hebrew and Christian Scriptures repeatedly sounds the coming of God's reign, God breaking into our lives, God calling us forth to life and labor. Our larger biblical inheritance is not an invitation to put God in our lives, but direct encouragement to be a part of God's continuing story, to cooperate with God in the work of creation generation after generation. Who we are matters within God's unfolding providence. In biblical parlance the quest for identity is intrinsically communal, belonging to a people rather than pertaining to isolated individuals.

We, like our biblical ancestors, carry more theology in our lives than in religious scrolls. This is a blunt observation with which to begin an expedition in religious understanding, but most journeys are marked by those we encounter along the way. John Bunyan's classic allegory of a Christian life, *Pilgrim's Progress*, repeats this emphasis. Bunyan's hero, Christian, proclaims: "The soul of religion is in the practic[al] part." Despite the frights and challenges of the Slough of Despond and battles with fearsome giants, Christian grasps a basic truth as he travels toward the heavenly city. Our responses to everyday events and persons we meet along the way inform and shape faithful Christian living. Ongoing coping and struggle, not dramatic highs and lows, are more likely to reflect the character, the soul, of religion.

Fortunately for those of us who are initially shy or experience trepidation when traveling, a practical pilgrimage is seldom solitary. Throughout my experience, personal and historical, I've known Christianity as a collective endeavor, a very human, often graced voyage destined at its best to invite widespread participation from all sorts of pilgrims. The central Reformation principle—which transformed European Christianity in the sixteenth century and today still enlivens peoples from many continents—is that faithful living takes shape within communities where all members, and not just a few leaders, struggle to understand and live out the faith. Whether we travel literally alone or with others, the mighty acts of Scripture and our worship tradition are common resources for wayfarers. Idealistic perhaps, yet this emphasis on the self shaped in relation to community has been understood by Christian pilgrims, peoples, and parishes throughout the ages. Rather than a how-to book for private struggle, I intend these reflections on commonly shared experiences as excursions for Christians in search of theological insight and direction for ourselves and our society.

Who Are We?

The search for spiritual identity, our basic self-definition, is seldom simple or painless. Like adolescents who learn about identity among their peers, religious seekers of all ages seem to be discovering in our own times that selfhood does not emerge in a vacuum. Ours is not the first culture in which individualistic how-to remedies have blurred and at times clashed with ancient expectations of holy living. The prophet Amos spoke to a people experiencing clashing values in the difficult transition from a society shaped by nomadic values to a settled, primarily agrarian culture. The first-century world of St. Paul was also characterized by fiercely competing, widely diverse political and religious allegiances. Yet Amos and Paul insisted that peoples, nations, and races were called to live according to harmonious, covenanted expectations.

3

They were clear that religious identity, while located in the hearts of individual men and women, was a collective, social pilgrimage, a journey in behalf of all people of God, including those unable to travel themselves.

Of course this quest for collective religious identity is easier described than lived. It is probably true for most of us that our sense of belonging to a wider community is not as well known or experienced as it was among our parents or grandparents. Today we are also left with the age-old problem of competing messages about identity. How can we think more constructively about this business of who we are as people of God in this modern world? What inherited resources address the struggles of daily living and ethical dilemmas of this age? Among others seeking spiritual enlightenment, what is the church's distinct identity? Are there significant ways of seeing, understanding, and doing things we can offer others? How do we continue our search for religious enlightenment living, as Christians do, among peoples of many and of no religions? Can we begin to define our terms in ways that directly increase our abilities to communicate across boundaries that seem to set us apart from others?

A search for religious identity that welcomes hospitality to others begins first of all with knowledge of our traditions and of the past. You might expect an historian like myself to turn to the past, to wisdom and stories from our ancestors. I find it is through immersion in conversation with past—as well as present—voices that we are able to learn our own religious inheritance, and find ways to communicate and identify with others. History involves overhearing conversations across the generations. History is about recalling ancient stories in the context of today's narratives. History involves a rabbinic mode of teaching: putting ancient voices in close dialogue with modern ones.

Recently I heard the modern theologian Raimundo Panikkar—a remarkable mystic and teacher of comparative spirituality—advise listeners from many religions: "You have to be who and what your are, concretely…in becoming concrete we discover that which is practical and universal." The reference to practical expressions of faith may seem odd given Panikkar's deep sense of universality. Yet Panikkar, like other mystics from St. Francis of Assisi to Annie Dillard, finds God's immanent activity in the concrete, not the abstract. His insight about mature religious identity reflects two principles: the imperative to know and to be deeply rooted in the spiritual truths of our own religious tradition, and the practical necessity of allowing this inheritance to inform responses to everyday experience.

There is a direct connection between the integrity of religious identity and the relevance of those contributions we are able to make in this world. Contemporary European theologian Jurgen Moltmann writes:

> The crisis of relevance and the crisis of identity are complementary to each other. Where identity is found, relevance is called into question. Where relevance is achieved, identity is called into question.[1]

To address these crises Moltmann lays a theological foundation connecting the struggles of today's world with our understanding of Christ's presence in our lives.

I find that the complementary character of identity and relevance is highlighted when we draw connections between everyday living and the Christian doctrine of the Incarnation. Like Moltmann, I have chosen to focus on the Incarnation because this biblical belief in a God who dwelt among us, human and divine, has been a guiding principle in Anglican thought and worship since the late sixteenth century, as well as a central Christian affirmation. Of course the doctrine of the Incarnation does not "belong" to Anglicans; all Christian creeds acknowledge that in Christ God has become human. Yet within Anglican thought there is a distinct tendency to put incarnational theology to use, to see ordinary aspects of human life through the lens of an incarnate God.

This book aims to bring late twentieth-century religious identity into focus by centering attention both on incarnational theology and on experiences common to most of us. I will concentrate on four aspects of human development: childhood, aging, work, and intimacy. These natural experiences lie close to God and to the heart of the study of God, which we call theology. These central experiences within the human life cycle are shaped as well by cultural and religious assumptions and messages about human identity, about who we are as we mature and grow in grace.

In these reflections I invite readers to understand theology in a newly embodied way. Theology is not an abstract system, but a way of life shaped in conversations that bring together reflections on God and common experience. Too many of us think that theology is "heady stuff" of use only to "experts." Instead, theology is critical reflection on our understanding of God, humanity, and the world. This book assumes that the theologies we espouse touch deeply upon familiar aspects of our lives. Implicitly and explicitly, Christianity is a living religion. Our theological identity, who we are, carries practical significance for everyday life.

What Do We Believe?

What do American Christians actually believe? It has been said faith crises come in threes. First, some Christians don't believe enough. Second, some Christians believe too much. And third, some Christians don't care either way. The central challenge is, What do we believe?

Modern Episcopalians are now able to address this question. Why? Because the dean of American polling, George Gallup, has completed a survey on religious beliefs and practices among American Episcopalians, and results are in about the Incarnation. Gallup indicates that seventy-seven percent of Episcopalians "strongly agree that Jesus Christ was fully human and fully divine," while as many as seventy-eight percent agree they find forgiveness of sins through Jesus Christ (others were less clear or did not express an opinion). When Christians, let alone Episcopalians, agree to this extent, we should all sit up and take notice. After all, these modern percentages about christological belief are far higher than those in 325, when the Nicene Creed was originally adopted! In any event Gallup concludes today's Episcopalians are "substantially orthodox" in religious beliefs, although he points to a gap between belief and "practice," by which he means involvement in their local churches.[2]

I want to point to a different gap: a gap between belief and knowledge. There is an African saying, "Not to know is bad. Not to wish to know is worse." I suspect many of us would admit to a gap between the affirmation of belief and a deeper understanding of the story's overall outline and meaning, between an assent to religious truth and the kind of understanding that invites us to put this knowledge to work. The most ardent Christian activist will acknowledge that thinking is an ongoing exercise in putting faith to work. At times I fear Episcopalians, like other Christians, have made a genteel accommodation to low-grade theological literacy. Supposedly Emerson once observed, "The merit claimed for the Anglican Church is, that if you let it alone, it will let you alone." It was of such behavior that Dorothy Sayers once coolly noted, "Many Englishmen would rather die than think, and many of them do."

Recently I asked a group of church people about the religious ideals and principles guiding their belief and practice. No one came close to mentioning the Incarnation. I was not entirely surprised. We can all pick the correct or orthodox response from Gallup's list of five options, yet we may not know or fully experience in our lives, our liturgies, or our work places what these affirmations claim on our behalf.

Believing and knowing are essential companions. Knowledge allows us to put information to work. This gap between believing and knowing suggests clergy and other Christian educators are overlooking the need to know, to hear basic information again and again. We may also be failing to learn theology in local parishes or to receive it as nourishment for daily living. I do not mean to be reductionistic—theology in all its dimensions does not have to be immediately useful or palliative. Certainly the radical biblical messages that shape expectations about responsible Christian living are seldom comforting to the status quo. Adults, like learners of all ages, are more likely to remember and make connections with information we find suggestive, pertinent, or even troubling in light of our own questions and contexts.

In ecumenical conversations Anglicans are traditionally known for thinking out loud, welcoming public theological debate. They are also recognized for the emphasis and attention they give to the Christian doctrine of the Incarnation. This indispensable Anglican tenet is built upon the New Testament witness of a God in Christ who came to live among us as God and as human. One European observer styled Anglicans as members of the "Church of Christmas Day." As early as 1623, when Anglicans moved to the Massachusetts Bay Colony, authorities responded to this unwelcome group by forbidding the celebration of Christmas. Historically, the Incarnation has been a particularly "extra-strength" doctrine in the hands of Anglican theologians, including those Archbishops of Canterbury who were also constructive theologians: Thomas Cranmer, William Temple, and Michael Ramsey. Michael Ramsey described the Incarnation as a critical principle for thinking about the inseparability of gospel and sacrament, humanity and God. In other words, the Incarnation is at the heart of Anglican theological interpretation.

Other theologians have also emphasized the significance of the Incarnation for Christian life and thought. D. M. Baillie of the Church of Scotland, writing about the same time as William Temple, reemphasized God's presence as the author of incarnation. In *God Was In Christ*, Baillie reminds us that when we speak of the Incarnation we are talking about God.

Chief among today's contributors in the interpretation of incarnational theology is a Roman Catholic, Jurgen Moltmann. He draws direct connections between the sufferings of Christ and those of the world. In *The Crucified God*, Moltmann insists that the atoning theology of the cross is an essential component in a theology of incarnation. Moltmann advocates living out incarnational theology within today's political contexts by seeking liberation for all humanity and by contending against situations of exploitation, oppression, and alienation.[3] Clearly this doctrine carries significant consequences for Christians, yet what does it mean?

As a child I observed two kinds of family members involved in sing-alongs: those who knew the tune but forgot the lyrics, and those who remembered all the verses by heart. Andrew Greeley, a Roman Catholic priest, journalist, and maverick author, remarks, "I have a theory that religion is experience in image and story, long before it becomes doctrine." This is true of the Incarnation, which first appears in the form of a story and not as a doctrine. For those of us who forget verses, what is the story of the Incarnation?

This story is found in opening of the Gospel of John:

> And the Word became flesh and lived among us, and we have seen his glory, the glory as of a father's only son, full of grace and truth....From his fullness we have all received, grace upon grace. (Jn. 1:14, 16)

The other gospelers add to this story in their implicit handling of the birth narratives and Paul from time to time mentions it in his writings. Yet it is clear throughout the New Testament that the special story of the Incarnation transforms early Christian experience of God, Christ, and the world. The modern Anglican theologian and bishop Stephen Sykes describes central aspects of this drama:

> The setting is human history, the theme is the rescue of mankind from destruction, the plot is the entry of

God into the context, and the resolution is man's judgement and final redemption.[4]

In the first instance the Incarnation is a recitation of Jesus' life, death, and resurrection. In its biblical fullness it is not only a nativity story, although we first hear of it at Christmas time. It is important to note when Anglican theologians refer to the Incarnation or (often interchangeably) to its derivative, incarnational theology, they are accentuating the fullness of Jesus' life, including his suffering and atoning death on the cross. The central principle is God in Christ's continuing self-identification with the human condition.

Obviously there is a lot going on in this dramatic story. The character of God is identified in vulnerable, concrete form; Jesus stands in unique relationship to God; God's presence in human life is irreplaceable. Well might we ask if there is one correct way of interpreting the Incarnation. The short answer is "no." Scholars, theologians, and bishops of the early church debated the precise meaning and definition of the Incarnation, each vying for the correct presentation of this doctrine. Their christological controversies led frequently to bloodshed, charges of heresy, and those hotly-debated confessional statements we now call "creeds." Bishop Sykes suggests that today every aspect of the biblical narrative, including the word "God," is open to searching questions and ongoing inquiry. In any church, disputes about interpretation are to be expected. One of several reasons for reading Scripture aloud in the liturgy is so all may hear the gospel and think for themselves. Defending one interpretation of the Incarnation as the only "correct" version would be close to idolatry. It would be similar to defending your own interpretation of a story as the only possible perspective.

Biblical writers, early Christian theologians, and contemporary scholars and theologians have in fact viewed the doctrine of the Incarnation itself as "a process of interpretation."[5] People in the past and the present have appropriated the Incarnation to see in new ways, raise new questions, and address new contexts. The Incarnation has inspired enlightenment among generations of Anglicans and other Christians. The seventeenth-century English poet and Dean of St. Paul's, John Donne, portrays rich incarnational insights in the fifteenth of his *Divine Meditations*:

> Wilt thou love God, as he thee? then digest,
> My soul, this wholesome meditation,
> How God the Spirit, by angels wait on
> In heaven, doth make his temple in thy breast.
> The Father having begot a Son most blessed,
> And still begetting, (for he ne'er begun)
> Hath deigned to choose thee by adoption,
> Coheir to his glory, and Sabbath's endless rest;
> ....
> T'was much, that man was made like God before,
> But, that God should be made like man, much more.

The Incarnation as "a process of interpretation" is far more than a narrow event. It reveals God anew and paradoxically helps us discover more concretely who we are. The French musician Olivier Messiaen, well known for his organ compositions, bluntly states in his meditation on the Incarnation, *Dieu Parmi Nous*: "The Word was made flesh and dwelt in me." This continuing process of interpretation allows us to speak of what one of my colleagues calls "the God-in-me-in-God."

The Incarnation has also served as a prism for looking at scientific and secular knowledge. Just over one hundred years ago a group of Anglican theologians, challenged by a whole new paradigm of ideals and theories about evolution proposed by Charles Darwin, turned to the Incarnation as a focus for delving into belief in their own day. The result was a series of brilliant essays published in 1889, *Lux Mundi*, the "light of the world." In his preface Charles Gore states several advantages to taking a fresh look at the Incarnation, among them the opportunity for contemporary readers to question what Christian faith really meant in their own day, explore whether faith was still adequate for interpreting daily life, and discover new moral and intellectual insights. Essentially the *Lux Mundi* authors spoke directly to what people of their day believed. Although many among their contemporaries were experiencing a crisis of faith, these constructive theologians, by daring to address the Incarnation alongside contemporary questions and challenges, animated and inspired confidence in the faith.

In a world undergoing major shifts, the Incarnation still holds power to create change, to inspire meaning, to reveal and challenge today's paradigms. I believe two things will begin to happen when we seek to understand human life in light of the images and insights of the Incarnation. We will be open to learning theology anew, seeking fuller understanding of God, humanity, and creation, and we will also discover timeless resources for interpreting today's contexts and crises. The contemporary American theologian Richard Norris insists that the doctrine of the Incarnation "compels us to ask whether God is a serious issue for us."[6] Through this question he wonders whether, in our struggles to come to terms with the world in practical ways, we express an ultimate meaning about the nature of God in Christ. In other words, reflection on the Incarnation prompts us to ask: what does Christian faith really mean in our own day?

Someone once remarked, "The trouble with good ideas is that sooner or later they require hard work." Will we move from believing to knowing—from surveys where we "strongly agree Jesus Christ was fully human and fully divine" to deeper expressions and understanding of God in Christ appropriate for our own time? Following the paths of our ancestors, our legacy is to accept this Christian challenge and assert that we are just the sort of people for whom this message of an incarnating "God with us" is definitive.

Theology is an Adventure

One of my faculty colleagues likes to envision theology as more of an adventure than a contest, since it is not suited to true/false answers or competitions with others. I think he is on to something. This teacher invites students into direct dialogue with early Christian forebears by asking them to write letters to them, so that Paul, Augustine, Jerome, and (I suspect) God have all from time to time been addressed via student dispatches. It is a pedagogy designed to break through the layers of distance and expectation of formal, stiff communication adults often bring to studying theology.

Sometimes I wonder whatever happened to the personal addresses of our childhood prayers, the "Dear God" notes, requests, and inquiries. Isn't it odd that as children we unhesitatingly asked "Why," yet for adults this standard plea for information seems too "forward." "And then what happened?" is the insistent response as I read a book to a young child. Questions like these allow us to continue telling the story. A child's interrupting pleas to know more about this or that can make a story read over and over appear fresh and new. Asking questions is one of the ways we join our own contexts to those in a book or text under study. The straightforward, unaffected, and direct inquiries of childhood remain excellent learning tools for pupils of all ages.

I suspect there are many thoughtful people who are drawn to the gospel yet are mystified by the doctrine of the Incarnation. So here's a significant adult question about the Incarnation: What does it really *mean*? What does it say about God, about God's view of humanity, and about our relationships with others in this world? Questions about meaning are different and, I would suggest, much more consequential than asking "What actually happened?" This latter question is shrouded in the mystery and paradox that always accompany our attempts to describe what God "does." Questions about meaning, on the other hand, can deepen our faith and our potential for faithful responsiveness.

The Incarnation provides a strong vantage point for this adventure into Christian faith. Through its prism we can rediscover the solid foundations of Christian theology. As the authors of *Lux Mundi* learned, taking a healthy look at the Incarnation helps identify what faith means. In this section I want to focus specific attention on four major theological components illumined by the Incarnation: the nature of God, the nature of humanity, the relationship of God and humanity, and the goodness of creation. Like four points of a compass, these topics can guide us toward new and renewed insight into our distinctive theological identity.

It is important to commence theological reflection on the Incarnation with pondering what it reveals about God. For although we may be more likely to consider what this doctrine purports for human life, the story of incarnation is first of all a statement about God's nature. It helps us explore what we mean by God. Images of God revealed in the Incarnation are those of an intimately engaged, concrete, and "worldly" deity. This is a God with a remarkable readiness to take on the conditions of mortal life, including vulnerability, responsibility, and risk. Through Jesus's earthly ministry, God becomes directly involved in humanity's suffering and joy. Christianity is the only world religion with a God who partakes of the fullness of human life. In essence, the Incarnation brings God to life, out of the shadows of abstract images, vague distant awareness, and Platonic ideals. In the Incarnation God becomes *expressible*. We are presented with not only the Word of God, but the Word made flesh. This is an active God who transforms reality by embracing it.

The Incarnation also reveals a God with sure commitment to humankind. The twelfth-century scholar and mystic Hildegard of Bingen expresses this movement in a haiku-like meditation:

> Divinity
> is aimed
> at humanity.

In this image, God seeks concrete engagement with humanity. Early Christian theologians held up this legacy. Augustine emphasized that the Incarnation represents a "new mode" of God's activity, which in effect narrows the gap between God and humanity. Centuries later two leading Reformation theologians, Martin Luther and Thomas Cranmer, would acknowledge Augustine's insight through their insistence on recognizing God's direct, saving intervention in human affairs.

Richard Norris also underscores how concrete God's ties are with humanity: "God objectifies himself for us in the life and death and new life of one human being."[7] God in Christ takes shape in one person. The ideal is not an abstraction, but a real human being. Because of the Incarnation, it is impossible to imagine a triune God who is distant, disassociated from humanity. This overall moral principle of God's direct involvement sets a pattern and inspiration for future ethical responsibilities. This principle, which we will explore in the following chapters, establishes the promise and reality of God's continuing self-identification with the human condition.

As a second point of identification, the Incarnation underscores the dignity and potential goodness of humanity. Its positive emphasis on human nature is distinctive. The collect for the Incarnation speaks of a God "who wonderfully created, and yet more wonderfully restored, the dignity of human nature." The English Reformation's greatest theologian and interpreter, Richard Hooker, believed that the Incarnation illumines the foundations of Anglican optimism: God's willingness to take on human flesh was "to better the quality" of humanity. Hooker explains that the intent of the Incarnation is to bring human nature closer toward conformity with God. We do not become identical with God, but rather move toward God's purpose and nature:

God has deified our nature, though not by turning it into himself, yet by making it his own inseparable habitation.[8]

In our own century Michael Ramsey, Archbishop of Canterbury from 1961-1974, concluded that the Incarnation was not only about God taking human flesh, but about human beings who are raised up to share in God's life. In other words, through the Incarnation God reveals human potential, coming nearer to the truth about humanity than we are able to see for ourselves. The image of an incarnating "God with us" establishes the optimistic promise Anglican theologians hold out for human life.

The result of these Anglican assertions about the nature of God and the nature of humanity, the theological "payoff," is a relationship of interdependence between God and humanity. "Interdependence" implies the willingness of both partners to change, to take on new, radical commitments. The philosopher Hegel believed the change wrought through the Incarnation allowed both divine and human to reach their apex; thus he describes the Incarnation as "the most weighty moment in religion." This two-way, interdependent movement brings humanity into deeper relation with God at the same time God is made man. The Incarnation closes the gap between a distant God and a lowly human race; divinity is aimed at humanity and humanity is raised up to share in God's life. In short, there is an identification of purpose, a pattern of strong mutuality.

This mutuality between God and humanity lies at the foundation of Anglican and Roman Catholic sacramental life. The sacraments both express and model divine and human cooperation and interdependence. Contemporary Roman Catholic theologian Leonardo Boff accurately points to a "courage for incarnation" that lies at the heart of all catholic Christianity, the courage to mix "heterogeneous elements" and to experience "the divine...made present through human mediation."[9] The courage envisioned here refers to God's initial courage in entering into the vulnerability and risk of human life, as well as to the courage of men and women seeking to live in the image of God. Even more so, I believe the Incarnation underscores the "courageous" relationship intended and expressed when both divinity and humanity accept responsibility for bringing forth God's reign in today's world.

The celebration of the eucharist, for example, both represents and nurtures our continuing responsibility to seek and to express God in Christ. In modern Prayer Book language, Anglicans do not blaspheme when praying that Christ "may dwell is us and we in him." The Incarnation provides the central theological foundation for Hooker's careful explanation of eucharistic theology because it models the cooperation of human and divine wills in God's redemptive purpose. This was one reason Hooker refused to accept the Lutheran concept of consubstantiation, which saw God and humanity actually joined together as one in the eucharistic elements. In the Anglican eucharistic liturgy, human and divine are *present* to one another; they cooperate rather than blur into one.

Holy Communion, Hooker remarks, is about changing human lives, not bread. Yet assumptions about God change as well. According to Hooker, the blunt truth confirmed in the eucharist is that without humanity God cannot "either exercise divine power or receive the glory of divine praise" (V.54.5). We might pause here for a moment to consider the implications of this stark Reformation claim. Do we really believe God's earthly reign comes into being without human responsibility? What do we expect God to accomplish in this world without human endeavor and cooperation? Do we truly believe in the transforming efficacy of eucharistic prayer? Hooker's bold assertion of radical mutuality expressed through the eucharist provides a distinctive Anglican perspective seldom mentioned in other Christian affiliations.

It also underscores God's intent in calling forth human goodness and responsibility. John Donne calls human beings "co-heirs" with God in expressing God's glory, while Jeremy

Taylor, another seventeenth-century Anglican divine, describes a partnership where human will and God's grace are not opposed. He speaks of directing our "actions to the glory of God" and God adopting these actions "as religion." In other words, we supply the intention or will; sanctification is God's doing. The Book of Common Prayer expresses a continuing eucharistic pattern of indwelling partnership when communicants give thanks for Christ's atoning death, and offer "our souls and bodies, to be a reasonable, holy, and living sacrifice" unto God. The images and ideals of the Incarnation provide the theological rationale binding God, humanity, church, and the sacrament of Holy Communion into an expectation about transforming the world by becoming directly involved in it.

This claim brings me to a fourth aspect of the Incarnation's transfiguring prism, the goodness of all creation. In the *Lux Mundi* essays Charles Gore concludes that the Incarnation places God in unique relation to all the universe, not only to humanity. We are misled if we think belief in the interconnectedness of all life and matter is a trendy "New Age" superstition. On the contrary, in the sixteenth century Hooker told us to rejoice in the whole creation. He believed that because God is present in all things, "all things that are, are good....nature is nothing else but God's instrument." The following sentence from a sermon by Hooker on pride is complex, yet its punch line is worth the effort:

> God has created nothing simply for itself; but each thing in all things, and of everything each part in the other has such interest, that in the whole world nothing is found whereunto anything created can say, "I need thee not."[10]

Nothing created can say, "I need thee not." The created universe yearns toward interdependence. The importance and worth of the creation is revealed by a God who chooses to dwell throughout creation. Earth and all earth-creatures represent the satisfying Genesis declaration, "God saw everything that he had made, and indeed, it was very good" (Gen. 1:31).

The evolutionary and ecological perspectives of Christians today have led more than one theologian to imagine the world as a metaphor for God's body. Contemporary theologian Sallie McFague envisions the world itself as metaphorically expressing God's presence. While it may seem a bit shocking, McFague believes it is urgent and necessary in an age threatened by nuclear destruction and marked by growing environmental decay to think of created order as part of God's incarnation. McFague is careful not to say the world actually *is* God's body, but to offer imaginative constructive ways of thinking about God and the world, ways which invite greater human responsibility and care:

> We can speak of God's incarnation in two ways: first, creation as a whole (God's body) is a sacrament or sign of the presence of God, and second, human beings...are sacraments or signs of God the lover.[11]

Both images—the incarnation of creation and the more familiar incarnation of God in Christ dwelling among us—express the theme of human interdependence with God's purpose.

McFague's insights should touch responsive cords among Anglican theologians who have emphasized both the goodness of nature and human responsibility for the created order. Anglican theology underscores God's continuing self-identification with humanity and with the earth God made. This incarnational emphasis directs us toward inspired participation in the unfolding potential of God, humanity, and our island home. It is in this context that John Booty, another prominent Anglican interpreter, describes Episcopalians as "environmentalists." Much as the *Lux Mundi* authors envisioned the Incarnation as bringing Darwinian insights into focus, so today theologians are bringing modern critical concerns

19

about ecology and the dangers of living in a nuclear age into dialogue with incarnational images.

Getting There is Half the Fun

Theology, which I define as a deeper understanding of God, humanity, and the world, is seldom an end in itself. Although we may need to dive deeper to discover new and renewed meaning in God's gracious presence, theological excursions need not be onerous. The Cunard Line once had a motto "Getting there is half the fun." I like to take a Cunard Line approach to theology, because good theology helps us keep on course and makes the trip more delightful. It can be an unforgettable part of the voyage. I find the allied wisdom of past and modern inquiry enjoyable and nourishing for the journey.

The Incarnation, literally "being in flesh," invites us to experience theology as intimately connected with our earthy lives. Perhaps it is useful as well to think about the "incarnation" of theology itself. How might we embody this doctrine in the style of today's culture?

A few years ago I was laboring (with only limited success) to express incarnational insights and images in conversation with a group of high school students. I suggested to them that we might construct signposts expressing what we felt about our faith, and we soon fell into the familiar, challenging pastime of thinking up bumper sticker "sayings." This mode of teenage evangelism was and is a way to recall, share, and travel onward with renewed insight. I have on occasion asked even adult learners to join in the fun. The following "bumper sticker" slogans are a shorthand way of summarizing clues to our theological identity.

#1. THEOLOGY IS AN EQUAL OPPORTUNITY EMPLOYER.

Reformation theologians insisted, "All can be theologians." Later William Law, an eighteenth-century theologian of great practicality, observed, "All Christians are by their baptism...made professors of holiness." A modern English bishop, J. A. T. Robinson, similarly remarked that theology is "too important to leave to bishops." People are participants, not observers, in Anglican theology. In the Prayer Book baptismal covenant we are reminded to continue "in the apostles' teaching." Accordingly this book and these "bumper stickers" are designed for all learners, lay and ordained.

#2. THEOLOGY IS NOT FOR COUCH-POTATOES.
Theology is an active noun. It takes hard work. In Anglican theology, along with a few sure answers, there are more questions than rules. If we think theology is a passive spectator sport, a game we ask others to play in our behalf, we are probably in the wrong denomination. Both our catholic sacramental heritage and the Reformation emphasis on "justification by faith" require our involvement.

#3. EXPERIENCE COUNTS...AND CHRISTIANS COUNT ON EXPERIENCE. This and the following bumper sticker speak to learners of all ages. Simply put, good education connects in some measure with our common thoughts and experiences. The concrete experience of the Incarnation, among other biblical stories, sets insights for future generations to follow in their own days. Our lives and engagements, then and now, matter. The connections we draw between traditional wisdom and current experiences and perspectives shape ongoing theological reflection.

4. THEOLOGY IS "AT HOME" AT HOME.
Theology is contextual. What we learn and how we live is often best expressed and represented within local language and societal patterns. Anglicans are, after all, ancestors of church leaders who turned sacred Latin, catholic liturgies into "common prayer" for a given national context. The Asian theologian C. J. Song notes that theology begins when it "identifies its home and discovers its belonging." I am not saying theology is culturally controlled, nor am I implying there are no universal theological principles. Certainly the Incarnation is a significant component of orthodox Christian doc-

trine. But I am suggesting that the ways we speak of God are always connected to a certain time and place. In fact, recognition of the unfolding historical nature of theology enlivens theological insight. As I've noted, one hundred years ago the *Lux Mundi* authors were called to speak of theology in the light of Charles Darwin's revelations. Today it is hard to imagine how our economic, social, and ecological concerns can be divorced from incarnational theology.

#5. CHRISTIANS "DO IT" WITH GOD AS A PARTNER.

The themes of mutuality of purpose and interdependence of activity suffuse the doctrine of the Incarnation. Love is love shown to one another and to God. God chooses to grow toward us as we strive to grow in love toward one another and toward God. A principal insight of incarnational theology is that God lives and loves among us.

#6. ANGLICAN THEOLOGY LIVES...AMONG US!

This play on "Che Lives!" graffiti of the 1960s is one of the most consequential principles of incarnational theology. "Living among us," the Gospel of John proclaims, "the Word became flesh." We carry more theology in our bodies than in our books. Theology is reflection on the living. Mother Jones once urged her contemporaries "to pray for the dead and work like hell for the living." If theology is a way of life, then doing theology involves reflection on human lives. Incarnational theology continues to take on new life when its insights and images are set alongside human experience. Consequently the central focus in the remainder of this book is upon human life.

In the following chapters I will reflect on our culture's current understandings of childhood, aging, work, and intimacy through the lens of the Incarnation. I have chosen these particular topics because they are too often taken for granted, if not flatly ignored, by most theological commentators. Moreover, there is urgency in addressing each of these aspects of daily life "in these United States," because each is approaching an implicit "crisis" status within our society. Statistical analysis of our demographic, familial, and generational profiles as a nation—and initial reports from the latest census about wealth and poverty—dramatically raise questions about young and old, rich and poor alike. In this analysis I have used the most recent demographic figures available, and as in-depth analysis of the 1990 census proceeds, even more information will be available for our reflection.

Statisticians are not the only ones examining childhood, aging, work, and intimacy in America. Contemporary social scientists are suggesting new ways for understanding these dimensions of human development. Much more attention, for instance, is being paid to America's youngest and oldest citizens. Thus I have intentionally chosen to address childhood and then proceed directly on to old age, rather than stopping to cover those topics in between. In part my intent is to highlight for our critical attention those two groups, the youngest and eldest of Americans, whose lives are often ignored amid our cultural overemphasis on autonomy and vigorous independence. By studying first the two extremes of the human life cycle, and then turning to topics more closely associated with our broad, middle years, I also wish to challenge implicit assumptions about developmental "progress" in mid-life. As we will see, there are biblical warrants for giving the youngest and oldest among us first priority.

In whatever order we take them up, these four dimensions of the life cycle are worthy of our best resources for sustained, critical theological reflection. Here's the challenge: can our understanding of theology and of humanity alike be enhanced by placing current socio-demographic data, perspectives, and reflections on children, aging, work, and intimacy in dialogue with the Incarnation? When recurrent realities of daily living are set alongside our central theological beliefs, will we be able to glimpse God, one another, and our joint responsibilities in new ways? These questions suggest a double focus: both what childhood, aging, work, and intimacy can teach us about the Incarnation, and how the insights and images of incarnational theology can inform our understanding of human experience.

My purpose is to stimulate further interest and, most of all, informed ethical perspectives and strategies. There are urgent ethical questions at stake. Perspectives on childhood in America raise alarming issues of hunger, endemic poverty, and abuse. How have we as a nation used and misused, supported or ignored our own and other children's lives and futures? An incarnational portrait of aging delineates God's abiding grace, but underscores as well those difficult, painful, and harshly negative dynamics that are too often used to depict and characterize our oldest citizens. The ambiguous matter of daily work raises questions of self-worth and individual justification, and reflects the changing occupational profile of workers in today's society as well as the continuing specter of unemployment. The enfleshed nature of human intimacy has long challenged and troubled theologians. Does the relational mutuality embodied in the doctrine of the Incarnation suggest more affirming patterns for our most intimate relationships?

At the heart of the Incarnation is the ideal of human wholeness, of helping us discover more concretely who we are and who God intended us to be. As with all theology, this book depicts potential divine and human interaction, offering insights about humanity and glimmers of God, the Holy One. These reflections invite us to examine what we believe and what we do. That the two should cohere is an abiding and troublesome biblical imperative that is difficult to follow and hard to fathom. While I intend to interpose constructively theology and human affairs, this is not a comprehensive theological survey of modern life, or a book of answers.

There is a true sense in which the supreme paradox of the Incarnation remains one of the mysteries of our faith. Although we cannot understand all that is meant, or do full justice to God's gift of love, Christians are invited in our collective lives of faith to express our identity courageously as followers of the Incarnate One. England's Cardinal Basil Hume once quoted a Greek orthodox theologian to illustrate the illusive, mystical nature of such a religious quest:

> You see, it is not the task of Christianity to provide easy answers to every question, but to make us progressively aware of a mystery. God is not so much the object of our knowledge as the cause of our wonder.

The "wonder years" of childhood provide a good vantage point to continue this incarnational quest.

Endnotes

1. *The Crucified God: The Cross of Christ as the Foundation and Criticism of Christian Theology,* trans. R. A. Wilson and John Bowden (New York: Harper & Row, 1974), p. 25.

2. "The Spiritual Health of the Episcopal Church," conducted by The Gallup Organization, 1989, and published by The Episcopal Church Center.

3. *Crucified God,* pp. 204-205 and 317-338; see also *On Human Dignity: Political Theology and Ethics,* trans. by M. Douglas Meeks (Philadelphia: Fortress Press, 1984).

4. Stephen W. Sykes, "The Incarnation as the Foundation of the Church," *Incarnation and Myth: The Debate Continued,* Michael Goulder, ed. (Grand Rapids, MI: Eerdmans, 1979), p. 123.

5. The continuing process of the Incarnation in our lives is underscored by Richard A. Norris Jr. in "Interpreting the Doctrine of the Incarnation," *The Myth/Truth of God Incarnate,* Durstan R. McDonald, ed. (Wilton, CT: Morehouse-Barlow, 1979), pp. 69-83, esp. pp. 73-75.

6. Ibid., p. 76.

7. Ibid., p. 79.

8. Richard Hooker, *Of the Laws of Ecclesiastical Polity* V.54.5. I have modernized quotations from Hooker, which are based on the original English of *The Folger Library Edition of the Works of Richard Hooker,* W. Speed Hill, ed. (Cambridge, MA: Harvard University Press, 1977).

9. Leonardo Boff, *Church: Charism and Power, Liberation Theology and the Institutional Church,* trans. J. W. Diercksmeier (New York: Crossroad Press, 1986), pp. 89, 92.

10. Richard Hooker, *Works,* 7th Keble edition (Oxford, 1888): 3.617.

11. Sallie McFague, Models of God: Theology for an Ecological, Nuclear Age (Philadelphia: Fortress Press, 1987), p. 136. See also her essay "The World as God's Body," *Christian Century* (July 20-27, 1988): 671-73.

2

Welcoming Children in My Name
Childhood in Incarnational Perspective

As a child I fell in love with church at Christmas. It is not the presents, the tree, or even the bitter-clear, snowy nights I remember from childhood, but the resplendent inside of my parish church. There was greenery everywhere, real candles on the choir stalls, a carillon and trumpets, and, most important of all, there were Christmas carols. How my mother and I sang in church! Singing was one way children participated in the long midnight ceremony and was our special treat, in unison and in harmony, verse after verse, carols old and new.

My mother, an actress, sang with gusto and lively expression. Later, when I was a young teenager, we invented a Sunday game called "Hymnal Chicken." Mother and I would hold our hymnals upside down. The loser was the first player who had to turn her hymnal right side up to recall the correct verse; winning skills usually combined memory and bluff. Much, much later on, the Christmas after Mother lost her voice to cancer, she pantomimed singing hymns by my side. Surprisingly, at the end of the service, a woman seated directly in front of us turned around and praised us for our lovely voices. I murmured words of thanks—Mother beamed—it was a magic moment.

Years later, a long journey from that memorable Christmas, it dawned on me I was imbibing theology through singing hymns. In effect "Hymnal Chicken" was catechesis, lessons in the faith. Singing hymns is for many children a way of learning theology; organists, choir directors, and other educators have known this for years. There is practical wisdom in the snippets of tunes and texts we find ourselves humming during the day. Robert and Nancy Roth, editors of a new children's hymnal, *We Sing of God*, speak of hymns helping children to "fall in love with God."[1] Hymns are doxologies of praise and mutual love. The music sung in our liturgies and remembered from our childhood is part of an ongoing love affair with God. Hymns provide an experience of "language" so that children and adults alike can explore God's presence. For children (and observant adults) they are living books of theology.

In my youth there was one very special hymn—a carol we sang at Christmas. This hymn inspired my early understanding of the Incarnation and my continuing curiosity about God's presence among us. The music for this lovely carol was written by Al Burt, who was related to one of our parish clergy. As a child of ten I committed to memory the words written by Wihla Hudson for Burt's carol, "Some Children See Him," words I can recall to this day:

> Some children see Him lily white,
> The Baby Jesus born this night.
> Some children see Him lily white,
> With tresses soft and fair.

Some children see Him bronzed and brown,
The Lord of Heaven to earth come down;
Some children see Him bronzed and brown,
With dark and heavy hair.

Some children see Him almond eyed,
This Saviour whom we kneel beside,
Some children see Him almond eyed,
With skin of yellow hue.
Some children see Him dark as they,
Sweet Mary's Son to whom we pray;
Some children see Him dark as they,
And ah! they love him too!

The children in each diff'rent place,
Will see the Baby Jesus' face
Like theirs, but bright with heavenly grace,
And filled with holy light.
O lay aside each earthly thing,
And with thy heart as offering,
Come worship now the Infant King,
'Tis love that's born tonight!

Make no mistake about it, this is a challenging text that is
rich in incarnational dimensions. There are several themes
here that reinforce the significance of the loving interdependence of God and humanity that is symbolized in the Incarnation. First of all, Burt invites us into a child's world of making
direct, personal connections. He recalls children's inclination
to identify others in terms of their own personal relationships: "What child is this?" asks another carol. Is this my
brother? Does he look like me, like a member of my family, a
relative, or is he a neighbor? The children of Burt's carol see
the baby Jesus as their own flesh and blood. As William Blake
wrote in his poem "Jerusalem," "He who would see Divinity
must see him in his Children." Incarnational identity, as we

noted earlier, is not abstract, and in Burt's carol it carries the particularity of a child's close connection to a God of love.

The carol also presents different children's images. Among "the children of each different place," there is a sense of incarnation profound enough to encompass and welcome racial and ethnic diversity, which is part of this carol's appeal and plea. I once asked my parents if Jesus was from Africa (I suspect Burt's carol put me up to it) and Mother's reply was, "Probably, yes." Seeing with incarnational identity is expansive, welcoming of all children, our own children and those of others, babes of many colors and hues.

"Some Children See Him" also reflects the Incarnation's power to transform expectations. Burt presents the baby as a personal bearer of God's grace, one whose face is "bright with heavenly grace, and filled with holy light." This is not a metaphor. This child is not only a gift of love, this child *is* love in human form: "Tis love that's born tonight." Christina Rossetti's nineteenth-century hymn elaborates,

> Love came down at Christmas,
> love all lovely, love divine.
> Love was born at Christmas:
> star and angels gave the sign.
> ....
> Love shall be our token;
> love be yours and love be mine,
> love to God and neighbor,
> love for plea and gift and sign.

Christianity at its best longs for the transforming love heralded in the nativity. The Incarnation reveals a God who partakes the fullness of life, beginning with the transforming love of a child.

Real-life children change and grow before our very eyes. So too Burt's baby Jesus is not only a newborn to be cherished, but a growing, living bearer of God's incarnate love. This theme of love freely given in this one child's nativity underscores the innocence and responsiveness of infancy. Burt's is not a sentimental view of childhood: new studies of morality in very young children emphasize their responsiveness to others and the basic ways they reach out, inviting and inspiring care. The words of the carol invite us to bring our hearts as a responsive "offering" to this child king. Much like the wondrous "Ah's" and "Ooh's" of children when they discover the delights of a nativity pageant, all who see the "baby Jesus's face" are invited to make their own expressions of love.

Modern authors confirm the sense of love and sacred awe inspired by children. Do you recall the scene from Alex Haley's *Roots*, where African American fathers affirm their child's place in the universe by holding up the newborn to the vast, starry sky and saying, "Behold the only thing greater than yourself." It is no wonder Virginia Woolf speaks of that "great cathedral space which was childhood." English moralist and author George Eliot similarly reflects, "We could never have loved the earth so well, if we had no childhood in it." A contemporary American scholar concurs, "In a secular age, children have become the last sacred objects." I see my preschool godchild, Tyler, as a sacred friend who moves commandingly in and out of my own life, regularly transforming my expectations about growth and creativity.

What have these "sacred objects" to teach us about the fullness of human life in the image of God's incarnation? This question is my focus for this chapter. What can we learn about the relational quality of life from reflecting on children as bearers of God's incarnation? Do their innocence and idealism have a place in society today? What can children teach us about our sense of connection to others, or about our use of power over those who are both vulnerable and innocent? After all, the circumstances of children's lives are largely dependent upon the good will and attention of adults. How do our expectations for the children close to us relate to our actions in behalf of other people's children? Children occupy an important place in thinking about these ultimate questions of value and purpose. Does our practical daily theology say anything about children? If not, can it be adequate?

I have spoken of the Incarnation as a process of interpretation that reveals God and humanity anew. When we start with the lives of children, we can see both ourselves and God's incarnation in a new light. While the remainder of this book focuses on other aspects of the human pilgrimage through the oldest age, developmentally the topic of childhood is a good place to begin focusing concretely on human lives. Yet it is very difficult to portray realistic perspectives on children. "Sacred objects" of all sorts and conditions are notoriously difficult to classify, and when reflecting on children adults are too often disposed toward sentimentality. It is risky to declare "children" a serious subject for mature reflection, since it can be trivialized on the one hand and romanticized on the other, and eventually dismissed as unworthy of critical attention. Perhaps this is why there are few professional theologians who have focused their—and our—attention on the lives of children. When we consider childhood, we are addressing a whole range of strongly-held assumptions, socially and culturally constructed "dos and don'ts." "It's obvious," one clergyman growled at me with gender assumptions galore, "you're writing only for women." In reply, I muttered that he was only half correct.

In this chapter, I am asking you to consider "childhood" as a mature theological topic. I want to invoke those private expectations most people have for the good health and success of their own children, as well as to encourage a public and shared commitment to welcome all children. If there are children in your immediate family, I am not only asking you to ponder your own relatives. If you belong as I do to the majority—the sixty percent of American households that are currently childless—I am asking you to think not only of a neighbor's child, or of your own childhood. All of these associations will help, of course, but my aim goes beyond that. Whether or not we are parents, grandparents, or godparents,

Christians are obliged to honor the earth's children. Perspectives on childhood are part of our basic theological identity.

In this country we are by all accounts moving away from the supposedly "child-centered" culture of the sixties and seventies, for, bluntly put, there are so many children in so much trouble in so many places in this nation. Commentators are pessimistic about children's lives in this and other countries, with foreboding implications. A new book by Richard Louv, *Childhood's Future*, talks about our nation's implicit and growing hostility to children. Alex Kotlowitz documents such hostility in his account of third-generation Chicago project children, *There Are No Children Here: The Story of Two Boys Growing Up in the Other America*. Similarly, Philip Greven's excellent new study, *Spare the Child: The Religious Roots of Punishment and the Psychological Impact of Physical Abuse*, reveals in what ways the historical beliefs, attitudes, and practices of Christians contribute to today's victimization of children.[2]

I was telling a friend of mine—a skilled elementary teacher who for twenty-five years now has taught scores of chiefly middle-class third-grade boys and girls—about what I hoped to accomplish in this chapter. "Tell them what it's really like," she said, "please don't spare the tough news." When I inquired further, this usually upbeat educator spoke with increasing dismay about the problems individual adults and our society as a whole are creating for her students: poor or no health care, malnutrition and hunger, lack of adequate childcare, and violence in the home and neighborhood. "How," she asked, "can I teach mathematical division to nine-year-old Anna in the morning, when I know she was sexually abused by her brother the night before?" Anna's story is not unusual, my friend insists.

As an historian I know that when we talk about childhood, we are not on neutral ground. Not too long ago historical study of the family was shunned by traditional historians, although the family has for centuries been a basic social unit.

Similarly, historical perspectives on "childhood" did not begin until the 1930s with Philippe Aries' *Centuries of Childhood*. Aries observed, and others have since confirmed, that for centuries children in most Western societies were either ignored or were defined in the negative as "miniature adults." Fortunately, childhood studies are now gaining status among social scientists. Can theologians remain far behind? The critical study of children is a hopeful, moral act. Here I have in mind Simone Weil's definition of morality as "the silence in which one can hear the unheard voices." What and who we choose to notice are reflections of our overall ethical stance as citizens and as Christians. Incarnational theology reveals a God who creates, risks, and embraces the fullness of human life—from the life of an infant in a manger to the lives of a young child like Anna and her troubled teenage brother.

Careful observation and patient self-critical listening are required if we truly expect to learn from children. Robert Coles, one America's most astute observers of children worldwide, presents stories and images from today's children in three recent books: *The Moral Life of Children, The Political Life of Children*, and *The Spiritual Life of Children*. This celebrated psychologist quotes Anna Freud on discovering what children persistently feel:

> Let us try to learn from children all they have to tell us, and let us sort out only later, how their ideas fit in with our own.[3]

This advice, necessary for purging ourselves of unwarranted assumptions about children, applies to learning from all those whose views are often dismissed or ignored. Listening can be proactive, leading to new solutions whether at home or in school. In a New York City church that runs an outreach project where volunteers and professionals work with children who have exhausted their teachers and frustrated their principals, one worker reports on his approach:

First of all you have to listen. When I start working with a child I don't know too well, I spend a lot of time listening to him before I try to suggest a course of study....So I listen until I have a sense of his particular problems, and then we work together to find out how to resolve them. That way he's already learning. He's analyzing his own problems.[4]

The feminist theologian and educator Nelle Morton advised her students and colleagues to "hear one another into speech." Listening, truly listening, to children is one way of honoring them in our midst. In the stories and descriptions of children's lives that follow, I invite to you to extend your understanding and commitment to children as an act of faith. Indeed, this essential theological topic is raised to prominence by God's direct entry into human life with the story of a child's birth. One of the ways children acquire information is by observing adults, and here we will observe *them*, hearing stories old and new of how "some children see him." In the process we adults can benefit from childlike curiosity, openness to discovery, and a desire for strong and loving ties with these offspring of God's love.

"The Bible Tells Us So"

Children are not new to Scripture. They have been there all along if only we knew how to look for them, as T. S. Eliot described in "Little Gidding" :

> And the children in the apple tree
> Not known, because not looked for....

Caring for the incarnate vulnerability and the potential of children is a biblical mandate. The Hebrew Scriptures are replete with dramas in which children figure prominently: the perilous river journey of the infant Moses and his watchful sister Miriam, the innocence of young Joseph and his brothers' treachery, or youthful David's courageous stand against Goliath. It is no wonder that those of us who were raised in parishes with vibrant Sunday schools found biblical stories exciting. My brother and I discovered that children actually were there, incarnate among our early Jewish and Christian ancestors, all along.

Yet what marks much of the Hebrew Scriptures' teaching about children is not found in dramatic tales of young persons responding to the mighty acts of God. In Israelite law codes children are repeatedly named among those deserving of God's special care and guidance. God is acknowledged as a loving parent and sure protector of the defenseless. The Covenant Code of the book of Exodus includes this injunction: "You shall not abuse any widow or orphan. If you do abuse them, when they cry out to me, I will surely heed their cry" (Ex. 22:22-23). The orphans of those days, as of today, may be taken to refer to any children who are abandoned—whether by relatives or by their larger society.

God is confidently praised in the psalms as the helper of the helpless, the poor, needy children, widows, and aliens. Accordingly, God strengthens the righteous "to do justice for the orphan and oppressed" (Ps. 10:18). The psalms also note that God rewards those who are devout with a large, long-lived, and prosperous family, one where parents live to see their "children's children" (Ps. 128:6). These and other scriptures encourage a normative ethic of adult responsibility for children, a society where it is unthinkable, an offense against God, not to care for children in need. "Who," as the Gospel of Matthew later challenges, "if your child asks for bread, will give a stone? Or if the child asks for a fish, will give a snake?" (Mt. 7:9-10). Being an advocate for children is a basic requirement of our biblical inheritance.

The gospels also present children as primary theological actors, critical to the unfolding incarnational drama of God's reign. This valuing of children was revolutionary, given the negative attitudes toward children in first-century Palestine. In the Greco-Roman world a child was considered unimportant, without status in the eyes of the world. A child could be the means of a family's survival (particularly if a son), but was without inherent worth. When food was scarce, it was not uncommon to leave children to die from exposure in the wilderness. Against this background the central point made in the gospels is not just that Jesus loved children, but that these "little ones" would help his followers see with the eyes of faith.

A crucial text, Matthew 18:1-5, reveals how children represent the knowledge of God in our lives:

> At that time the disciples came to Jesus and asked, "Who is the greatest in the kingdom of heaven?" He called a child, whom he put among them, and said, "Truly I tell you, unless you change and become like children, you will never enter the kingdom of heaven. Whoever becomes humble like this child is the greatest in the kingdom of heaven. Whoever welcomes one such child in my name welcomes me."

"Whoever *welcomes* one such child in my name welcomes me." I much prefer the New Revised Standard Version of the Bible, which here replaces the familiar word "receives" with the more active and accurate verb "welcomes." In their own way Mark and Luke repeat this emphasis: when we greet children in God's name, we welcome the Incarnate One in our midst. The lives of the youngest and least powerful among us represent divine priorities. Children lead us to God's presence and among them is this measure of greatness to be found. I think the point is also being made that adults and children are not the same; however much we "grown-ups" think we understand children, many of us have forgotten what it was like to *be* a child. Children in these stories are to be welcomed on their own terms, not only when as mini-adults they are obedient to our rules. These Bible passages teach us lessons about power, about the vulnerable ones who, despite their fragility, are "the greatest."

The teaching of Jesus of Nazareth models far more than hospitable care for children. The key theological message is underlined in a second passage from Matthew:

> Then little children were being brought to him in order that he might lay his hands on them and pray. The disciples spoke sternly to those who brought them; but Jesus said, "Let the little children come to me, and do not stop them; for it is to such as these that the kingdom of heaven belongs." And Jesus laid his hands on them and went on his way. (Mt. 19:13-15)

Mark and Luke repeat the news "It is to such as these [children] that the kingdom of heaven belongs." Children are *the* quintessential members of God's realm. They are signs of God's expected reign, heirs of the unmerited gift of grace. For Matthew, who is the most dedicated of the gospelers to the biblical metaphor of transformation through God's impending reign, children are pleas and gifts and signs of God. These most vulnerable members of society are the most welcomed heirs.

Two more manifestations of God's incarnation are underscored in New Testament teachings about childhood. In Luke's compelling infancy narratives it is clear that the Incarnation is a model of growth and transformation. In Luke alone the young child grows before our eyes. The stories are brief but telling: from birth and swaddling clothes, to circumcision and purification, and on through early childhood Luke records, "The child grew and became strong, filled with wisdom" (Lk. 2:40). This is followed by the remarkable episode of Jesus' presentation in the Temple as a twelve-year-old, listening, questioning, and sharing his learning with those teachers who were the local experts in the Jewish religion (Lk. 2:41-51).

This trip from Nazareth to Jerusalem's Temple, along with family and friends, was more than an exhilarating adventure. Here is a glimpse of incarnation that involves growing up, but not, as is often the case, as a sentimentalized concept. Growth in this story partakes of the fullness of human life; it includes making choices, sometimes painful ones between a parent and a child, and taking responsibility in new and challenging circumstances. In Luke's narrative the young Jesus, like the children in our own lives, changes before our eyes, gaining in wisdom as well as physical strength. Incarnational theology models not only new birth, but sure expectation of growth and transformation.

One other story, taken from Matthew's quite different nativity story, points to God's readiness in the Incarnation to take on the fullness of mortal life, including vulnerability, risk, and the tragedy of young children's deaths. Matthew's story of the birth of the child Jesus includes infanticide, a story that he alone tells. Matthew's depiction of the slaughter of innocents, when an infuriated Herod "sent and killed all the children in and around Bethlehem who were two years old or under" (Mt. 2:16), dramatically juxtaposes the themes of power over dependent children, vulnerability, and innocence. In the face of such terror, Matthew recalls Jeremiah's prophetic expression of grief:

> A voice was heard in Ramah,
> wailing and loud lamentation,
> Rachel weeping for her children. (Mt. 1:18a)

Anglican theologian Charles Williams said of the slaughter of the innocents:

> There is no more significant or terrible tale in the New Testament than that which surrounded the young Incarnacy with the dying Innocents.

This story ought to put to rest any doubts you might have about the costly character of God's incarnation. With Rachel's weeping in our ears, we can recall the profound character of God's direct intervention in human life. Sweetly romanticized visions of the baby Jesus' nativity, common in "Christmas card theology," are too shallow a prophecy for the real lives of children then and now. Paradoxically, the birth of Jesus dreadfully underscores the fragility of other children's lives. New Testament mandates about welcoming children include not only provisions for protective hospitality, but also challenge adult expectations about worth and greatness, and recall scenes of grief as well as joy.

The incarnation of the Messiah, of God's Child, does not herald an easy peace. It does, however, direct us toward a more promising age. Much as this Child's birth provides reasons for hope and promises to be fulfilled, all children at their birth can provide reasons for hope, for a life of unlimited possibilities. Zechariah, the colorful sixth-century prophet of the messianic age, describes the promised reign in these terms:

> Old men and old women shall again sit in the streets of Jerusalem, each with staff in hand because of their great age. And the streets of the city shall be full of boys and girls playing in its streets. (Zech. 8:4-5)

This too is part of the promise, an aptly incarnational, intergenerational vision of the new Jerusalem in which children not only survive, but prosper along with their ancestors. For those who see through the eyes of faith, God's promises to the children of the new Jerusalem for a peaceful and a more gentle time signal our responsibility to welcome children into a world in which they, too, are free to play in the streets.

"Other People's Children"

Most parents hold on to promising dreams for their offspring. We want the best, and make sacrifices for our own. Thus when we read debates about child-raising and statistics on children as a demographic class, most of us look at this data in the context of our immediate families. My adolescent nephews, my preschool godson, and my students' young children come quickest to mind. These personal friends and relations are incarnate references for measuring what is happening in this country. They provide, or so I used to believe, an adequate template for reconsidering America's children.

A recent journey to Brazil changed this perspective. I was traveling to the Brazilian city of Salvador for a church conference. Ostensibly I was there to work side by side with adults from the global Anglican Communion to respond to the Ecumenical Decade of Solidarity with Women. Yet I did not anticipate the role children would play in the real fabric and theological soul of these deliberations. For most of us this was not a first glimpse of the other side of affluence, though few of us will be able to forget Salvador's impoverished children.

Local authorities had tried to sweep the streets free of begging children (much as they did later for the Earth Summit in Rio de Janeiro). Indeed, a workshop speaker told us of street children who were hunted down and shot; a local bishop confirmed such reports. Yet some children survived this modern-day slaughter of the innocents. Wherever we walked, there were little boys, pointing to their mouths and pleading, "Mon-ee, Mon-ee por favor!" Spindly, stick-figure little boys clamoring and dancing around us; little girls (we later learned) who survived starvation would later take their turn on the streets as young prostitutes. Meanwhile in a conference plenary session, a UNICEF representative talked about the forty thousand children who die every day worldwide and emphasized the desperate need for "child-friendly" health clinics and hospitals. The odd phase tripped me up—it had never occurred to me that hospitals would be "unfriendly" to sick, malnourished children.

Iris Murdoch once wrote that the entry of a child into the story changes the whole situation. The plight of Brazil's street children, not just the statistics, but the children we saw and touched every day, converted my image of the church. By the time I'd left Brazil, my spiritual home was not Canterbury and its distinguished-looking English prelates, but Brazil, whose street children with pleading smiles had become the present incarnation of today's biblical texts. It was as if these Brazilian children had been deliberately set in our midst by some latter-day Matthew to recall what the reign of God was all about. Our task was to welcome them, not just as Brazil's children but as our own. Seen through the eyes of faith, these were not "other people's children," but flesh and blood in the family of God.

Jonathan Kozol has directly informed my reflections on "other people's children." His recent book on American schools that are "unfriendly" to children, *Savage Inequalities*, focuses on young lives starved in body and mind, children living in impoverished third-world conditions in the United States. Kozol exposes the stark questions at work in the formation of public education policies—questions about whose children get to eat before school begins, about who shall be educated to what level and in what kind of buildings, and, most pointedly, about how much we have to invest in *this* child as opposed to *that* one. What type of disparity in schooling, in nutrition, in health care or emotional support should be permitted between our own children and those of others?

William Temple, a prophetic mid-century Anglican archbishop and theologian, in *Christianity and the Social Order* bluntly asked:

> Why should some of God's children have full opportunity to develop their capacities in freely-chosen occupations, while others are confined to a stunted form of existence?

Temple insisted that for Christians to act on behalf of "purely personal relationships" was not enough, and in public affairs he urged contemporaries to subordinate their own self-interest to that sector of society which was "evidently in greater need." Welcoming "other people's children" as well as our own underscores Temple's expansive vision of incarnational theology.

As I "listen in" on children's lives in this country, I have comes across not only reflections and stories about individual children, but also information from statistical abstracts, community and governmental reports, psychologists, pediatricians, scientists, journalists, and teachers. Many creative researchers today are reconsidering and revisioning childhood. My task, drawing from their learning, is to present a contextual picture of American children—our own and those of others—for our theological reflection.

This brief summary of recent socioeconomic and demographic data about children focuses on large-scale trends. The largest of these is the fact we are in the middle of a "baby boomlet." Not surprisingly, the so-called baby boom children of the post-World War II decade are now bearing their own children. By the mid-1990s there will be twenty-three million preschoolers, which is only one to two million fewer than the highest figure for the 1950s. Statisticians employ humorous figures of speech, calling the current situation a "baby boom echo." The play on naming, however, is about all this generation of children now growing up in the United States has in common with their parents' childhoods. Today's youngsters face another world in every economic, racial-ethnic, and geographic circumstance. "Boomlet" families are increasingly multiform because of divorce and remarriage, cohabitation, diverse lifestyles, and the increased number of single-parent families.

A second major trend is childhood poverty. This country may now be first in the number of billionaires; sadly, we also come first among industrial nations in childhood poverty. The income of young families declined steadily through the 1980s. Before I began to gather these figures, I thought that the proliferation of two-income families was helping them keep up with basic expenses. The fact is, although over sixty percent of women with children under six are now employed in the work force as well as unpaid workers in the home, real family income remains below 1973 levels. This shocking fact is just the tip of the economic iceberg: in 1986, over thirteen million children lived below the federal poverty level and this number is growing. The new 1990 census reveals that one in four Americans under the age of eighteen is poor. Children are twice as likely as adults to live in poverty.

Having an employed parent or even two does not mean children escape poverty. Among two-parent families living below the poverty level, forty-four percent have at least one full-time worker. Poverty is particularly high (sixty percent) in female-headed households; this should not be surprising, since a single mother with just one child working a full-time job at a minimum wage cannot earn enough to escape poverty. In all, the youngest families in this country are most at risk. The stress on parents who are trying to provide both economic support and adequate care for their children is likely to intensify. One prediction for the year 2000 is that at least half of all children in the United States will have spent some or all of their childhood in poverty, a prophecy that bears rereading and pondering.

Some children are more in danger than others. The Federal Government reports that there are at least twelve million children without any health care at all. Currently one out of two African American children and two out of five Hispanic children are poor. A disproportionate number of poor white children live in rural areas, where, since 1978, poverty has grown twice as fast as in urban sites. Although less than a decade ago a federal official said there was "no authoritative evidence of hunger" in America, a 1991 report identifies 5.5 million children under twelve—that is, one out of eight—who go to bed hungry, while an additional six million are at risk. An eight-year-old child testifying before a House Committee brings out the poignancy of these statistics:

> When I grow up I will be president of the United States...then everyone will have a little money in

their pockets. And no little boy like me will have to put his head down on his desk at school because it hurts to be hungry.[5]

In *Savage Inequalities*, Jonathan Kozol tells of small children putting chicken nuggets from the school cafeteria in their pockets on Fridays because they are afraid of being hungry over the weekend.

There is a third trend, one we are recently noticing in the aggregate: the astounding incidence of child abuse. Tragically, families are not always safe or trustworthy places for children. Children live amid an epidemic of family violence and neglect. On one day in the lives of America's children, almost two thousand youngsters are abused or neglected. It is difficult to overestimate the importance of adult "good will" toward children when at least one in three females and one in eleven males are sexually abused before the age of eighteen. Nine out of ten times the perpetrator is a family member or another person known and trusted by the child.[6] Anna and her teenage brother are not isolated examples.

Another painful aspect of this epidemic is the fact that children are increasingly taught to accept, however shameful, violent behavior. Benjamin Spock believes this is the most significant change to occur in children's lives since he published his first book on child-raising in 1946. Reports of family violence make it clear many adults think children have few rights or merits of their own. For example, one of the most pervasive assumptions many Americans continue to defend is their "right" to discipline children through corporal punishment. In *Spare the Child*, Greven poignantly illustrates that when we deliberately hurt children, we actually teach children to hurt themselves and others. Greven confesses that as a parent he occasionally succumbed to spanking "as a last resort," but now he has changed his mind. Along with Dr. Spock, he now advocates other and much more effective forms of discipline.

The pain children experience in this violent society is not only physical. Psychologically, a child in America today receives less family time and attention than in prior generations. Among the children of wealthier parents, Marian Wright Edelman of the Children's Defense Fund describes a bug of "affluenza" contracted by children in families who offer much that money can buy, but fail to create a sense of purpose in their lives. She concludes that a whole generation of children are at risk:

> Millions of children are not safe physically, educationally, economically, or spiritually and on the average poor and members of minority groups are less safe than their white, more affluent counterparts. But all are at risk spiritually.[7]

Such trends, whether in this country or in Brazil, are plainly difficult to hear, and Robert Coles suggests at times we protect ourselves from being deluged with such tragic facts by "psychic numbing." It is not a new phenomena to distance ourselves from hard realities; long ago the prophet Amos railed at his contemporaries' inability to appreciate the predicament of the poor. T. Berry Brazelton, who like Dr. Spock is a popular and knowledgeable "baby guru," reports that when he speaks of the problems of two-career middle-class families, the news media are attentive; not so with poor families. "News of impoverished families" is an oxymoron. Even if we are able to move beyond the guilt, complacency, and the "It-couldn't-happen-to-my-family" reflex, there is an implicit social bias in this independent-minded culture against helping out low-income families "who ought to be making it on their own." What will happen, columnist Ellen Goodman asks, if "the staggering facts" about our children and their young families no longer have the power to stagger us?

We are not without solutions. The 1991 report *Beyond Rhetoric: A New American Agenda for Children and Families* from the bipartisan National Commission on Children focuses on proven ways to support children at risk within family and community contexts. Similarly, another report from the Committee for Economic Development—a group of 250 leading business executives—calls for "swift and decisive" investment in our nation's children. They maintain, and organizations like the Children's Defense Fund and the National Commission on Children confirm, that we know what measures work in alleviating poverty among young children and their families. They detail "financially possible" efforts that would cost about ten billion dollars a year—roughly the cost for two weeks of Operation Desert Storm. Meanwhile, for church groups interested in supporting children, the Children's Defense Fund has issued a timely and helpful resource that presents practical, accessible ways parishes can make a difference called *Welcome the Child: A Child Advocacy Guide for Churches*.[8]

Moving from what we know to what we can do is never easy. Marian Wright Edelman suggests children are this nation's poorest citizens because we adults have lost our moral bearings. Creating a moral climate for welcoming children is a matter of moral responsiveness and will power. Have Christians, among other Americans, forgotten what these "greatest ones" in our midst have to teach us about innocence and vulnerability, about interconnectedness, and about respecting God's incarnating presence in our own and other people's children? What clues to our adult dilemmas about child-raising can be found in children's lives?

"Some Children See Him"

A cartoon from the *New Yorker* shows a woman deep in conversation at an elegant cocktail party who asserts, "My latest book is for three-to-five-year-olds, but I like to think there's something in it for everyone."

I would like to think that a theology of childhood would be a valuable resource for us all. What would such a theology look like? Would it include pieties and platitudes that are common adult fare? Probably, yes. I don't know for sure, of course, because a true theology of childhood, one deeply informed by children's lives, needs to be shaped by children themselves. Yet as a grown-up I am able to identify distinct theological emphases in the lives of my younger friends, including the things they have to teach us about God. I suspect too that a theology of childhood, like most good theological reflection, is not static; instead, it combines continuity with motion and transforms the expectations of those who experience its power in their daily lives. No doubt it also honors the persistent asking of questions, including ultimate questions like: Where do we come from? Why are we here? Where are we going?

In constructing a theology of childhood it is important to turn to children and to those researchers who grant them the status of participants and constructors of their own world. Chief among these is the child psychologist Robert Coles, whose interviews with children about their moral, political, and spiritual impressions bring youthful words and images to life. Like Coles, professor of education Carol Gilligan and her colleagues are rethinking childhood by listening to children and adolescents, encouraging them to express and learn from their own voices. Their research promises new visions of childhood where children are welcomed as authorities in their own lives. I have drawn samples of new perspectives from this extensive literature which, when combined with children's impressions of God, illustrate central motifs in an emerging theology of childhood.

A key characteristic of a theology of childhood, and one we observed earlier in Luke's stories about the child Jesus, is the expectation of growth and transformation. Every time I see my nephews, they have changed in some way. They are not only taller, more articulate and challenging; they seem to become, before my eyes, more of the persons God intended them to be. So too, according to Coles, children's pictures of God, indeed of God's incarnation, represent change and openness to transformation. A nine-year-old carefully explains the movement in her crayon drawing of God:

> When God came here, He looked like a man; He was Jesus, But then He went back to being God, and I don't know what He looks like now....I'm not sure I should finish [my picture].[9]

This child's awareness of growth and willingness to wait for new images of God not only reflects who children think God is, but also mirrors their understanding of who they are. A child in a fifth-grade classroom wrote, in response to Coles' question "What makes you the person you are?"

> I'm like I am now, but I could change when I grow up. You never know who you'll be until you get to that age when you're all grown. But God must know all the time.[10]

Children confirm that God and humanity alike grow in newness of life.

I am confident that a second component in a theology of childhood would be social responsiveness. Researchers are discovering that babies learn more rapidly than we adults previously admitted. As early as seven months, one study concludes, children can recognize a human face as more than a combination of parts; at eighteen months they can comprehend the reasoning behind each step in taking a bath. These observations call into question psychologists' prior assertions that children do not think conceptually until they are seven or eight years old. New studies document young children, including infants, are basically socially responsive, appreciative of others, and capable of altruism.

This material challenges older views of an infant's nature as egocentric, asocial, amoral, and capable only of parallel or imitative play. Jean Piaget's influential 1930s assessment of the significance of a young child's social life is being recast: from the view that individual children left to themselves *re-*

main egocentric, we have moved to the new belief that children who are left to themselves *become egocentric*. Piaget was correct about the formative importance of interpersonal relationships in early childhood development; what he underestimated was the infant's fundamental relational identity. When, for example, an infant reaches out to touch a parent's face, we can observe growth as responsive movement toward, and not away from, others.

Prior assessments of very young children overlook not only their basic appetite for social relations, but also the responsive power of imagination and creativity. Play is the third and leading component in a theology of childhood. Children like to pretend—most of us know that. Recent research indicates young children need to play as much as they need to relate to others. Studies of toddlers (ages fifteen to twenty-four months) playing with their mothers surprised researchers by showing the first sparks of imagination usually come from the child, not the adult. Children's imaginations light up during active mother-toddler play when the child takes the lead, while parent-directed play shuts down creativity. Toddlers' minds, like everyone else's, flourish when they are neither bossed around nor ignored. Even the youngest children learn by fashioning their own responses. Children remind us that imagination and creativity are important responses to life in God's image.

Gabriel Moran, whose valuable books on religious education repeatedly capture my attention and imagination, once observed that "play...embodies the child's attitude to the sacred."[11] Playing with stories and with ideas, testing their limitations and exploring the absurd, are part of learning. Perhaps this is one reason the books of Dr. Seuss (my godson's favorite author) delight children (and many adults) worldwide. In Dr. Seuss's books imagination is a child's natural ally in a world full of chairs that are too big. For those who feel as small as a speck of dust in an elephant's hand, Dr. Seuss in *Horton Hears a Who!* reminds us, "A person's a person. No matter how small." We learn from children's playful imagination that it is possible to think about the meaning of life and laugh at the same time.

The experience of adolescence has theological implications, too. Forming close connections with others is another emphasis within a theology of childhood. Similar to studies that re-vision the interpersonal capabilities of infants and young children, the work of Carol Gilligan and her research colleagues is questioning and reforming prior assumptions about adolescents. Their research with adolescent girls points to the significance of strong, caring relationships. Psychologists have traditionally described the adolescent "crisis" as a struggle for separation and autonomy, a choice between being "selfish" and "selfless," but Gilligan observes that to see "self-sufficiency as the hallmark of maturity" presents "a view of adult life that is at odds with the human condition."[12] Gilligan's studies show adolescent girls experience crisis not because they seek autonomy, or have to choose between self and others. Rather they are struggling, in the face of "a wall of prohibitions" about becoming "a woman," to stay connected with themselves, with others, and with their world.

Adolescence is a critical time for gaining moral perspective. Studies by Gilligan and her colleagues document a pattern they call "co-feeling," whereby adolescent girls acquire sensitive and increasingly mature skills in human interaction. Co-feeling is the capacity to experience feelings different from one's own, to identify, for example, with other people's children:

> Co-feeling implies an awareness of oneself as capable
> of knowing and living with the feelings of others, as
> able to affect others and to be affected by them.[13]

Co-feeling is distinguished from empathy because it expresses engagement with others rather than judgment or patronizing observation. Gilligan suggests that young girls who are moving into adolescence should be supported in maintaining caring connections with themselves and others. When these feelings are suppressed, the result can be detachment and passivity and, more tragically, such misguided strategies to "care" for themselves as early pregnancies, eating disorders, and even suicide. Gilligan argues that adolescent identity is formed not by separation, but by gaining perspective through hearing different voices and points of view.

Much as social responsiveness expresses the origins of morality in young children, co-feeling in adolescents points toward their concern for maintaining relationships and resisting the temptation to turn away from those in need. Coles' respondents express co-feeling in their pictures of God, as in a drawing by a nine-year-old African American girl who chose to depict God in action:

> When He saw someone in trouble, His heart skipped a beat....He'd see someone, and he's stumbling and he might be blind, and Jesus could feel just the way the man felt, blind Himself, and He'd get right in there, and try to get the man back to seeing....Maybe [she adds] Jesus sang while He healed.[14]

Another youngster observed, "If you are really remembering Jesus, you remember the people he wanted to help."

Overall, Coles' observations of individual boys and girls reinforce Gilligan's emphasis upon the value children place on staying connected with others and being true to themselves. He is convinced children start out as moral pilgrims. Whether in Mississippi, Soweto, Nicaragua, or Belfast, children lead profound moral and political lives. They struggle daily to make sense not only of how the world works but how it "ought" to work. For example, they integrate external tragedies directly with events in their own lives. Children in Belfast respond to hunger strikes in the Maze prison by becoming preoccupied with their own eating habits, while "colored," mixed race children in South Africa draw themselves in violently clashing colors. Coles' blunt conclusion warrants further meditation in light of the violence and other risks children face in this country: "A nation's politics becomes a child's everyday psychology."[15] As Coles and Gilligan concur, children are neither apolitical nor amoral. Instead, these young generations hold the promise of moral wisdom.

No wonder children and adolescents are often characterized as idealistic, while adults who insist on social responsiveness and moral concern for others are sometimes caricatured as "delayed adolescents." I do not mean to present a contrast between overbearing, unresponsive adults and innocent, saintly children, for of course children can be cruel, selfish, and self-centered. Yet the question remains: are idealism and the moral insight of many children traits adults must grow out of? The sense of connection to others actualized in early childhood, and represented in incarnational theology, is a basic human characteristic. Children, I believe, challenge "grown-up" theologies to reappropriate care and moral connection in more profound ways.

Children's theological reflections include reflection on life's value and purpose. Listening in on stories from Hopi, Israeli, Pakistani, and African American children, Coles found that religion fosters cohesion and wholeness in their lives. Even children who are not from religious families do a lot of thinking about God. A ten-year-old child of atheists insists:

> Just because you don't go to church and don't believe what they tell you [there] doesn't mean you don't think about God, and about how you should be good, what are the really big things in life, and the things that don't make any difference.[16]

What children think about God indicates that even young children know that growth involves making purposeful choices, perhaps painful ones, with an eye to the future. A young girl confidently shares her convictions with Coles:

I don't want to waste my time here on this
earth....When you are put here, it's for a reason. The
Lord wants you to do something. If you don't know
what, then you've got to try hard to find out what. It
may take time. You may make mistakes. But if you
pray, He'll lead you to your direction.[17]

Children look for purpose in life, for a "larger picture" of
things, for a sense that they are part of a process with an "earlier" and a "later."

Incarnational perspectives on childhood also challenge
normative assumptions about adult control of children's lives.
When we reflect on power dynamics between children and
adults, we are faced with a conundrum. It is perhaps easier to
envision mutuality and interdependence among adults than
among children and adults. Do we have to shift incarnational
expectations of interdependence when dealing with innocent
and vulnerable children? I think not, although we do need to
be realistic because interactions between adults and children
involve both attachment *and* inequality. Children are intimately aware of being smaller and less capable than adults
and older children, yet they are nourished by adult abilities
and expectations. Obviously they are not fully independent
creatures, nor is their identity entirely dependent upon
adults.

One author accurately describes this interdependent relationship as marked by contingency. Children's circumstances
are largely "contingent on the good will of adults."[18] The root
of "contingency" comes from the Latin word for "touching."
Contingency implies a connection which, while it may not always remain the same, is important nonetheless. It connotes
responsibility. Parents in fact have a far greater role to claim
than "taking power over" their children. Adults and the children they love have the power "to touch" one another's lives.
Inequality and attachment are honored components in a theology of childhood that takes questions of power seriously.

The consequences of exercising power over children's lives can be seen in our parishes as well as our homes. I remain haunted by a story I heard this past Easter from a parent whose five-year-old daughter sobbed most of Easter Sunday. The priest (a relative newcomer and a strict disciplinarian) had refused to give this child communion when, recalling her parents' explanation about being fed at the church's "family table," she had put out her hands at the altar rail. This young girl (like most children) knew when she was not wanted, and later told her mother she must have been a "very, very bad girl." Just what is the "everyday psychology" for children in parishes?

What kind of power, for example, do parishes exercise over those children in their midst? Do we truly welcome children, or do they have to behave like "miniature adults" to attend services? When adults, including parents, suggest that they don't want to be "disturbed" by their children during church, isn't it time to reexamine theological assumptions about both worship and children? Did you know that it was common practice during the first thousand years of the Christian church to communicate all baptized infants? Anglican liturgist Leonel Mitchell insists that the central reason to communicate infants is not for their benefit alone; rather, it is a sign to the church and wider community that these little ones are witnesses of God's unmerited grace, a theological emphasis our Protestant Reformation ancestors would have liked as well.[19] More, of course, could be said about welcoming children in congregations. Yet the central point I wish to make is that welcoming children in our midst recalls gospel mandates about exercising power with care and consideration for all God's children.

Lastly, I am sure the children in my life would insist that a theology of childhood is intergenerational as well as interdependent. My nephews, for example, love to hear stories "from the olden days" when their daddy was a child, stories that stretch all of our imaginations. Gabriel Moran wisely

points to the "natural alliance" between the very young and
the very old:

> The most dramatic embodiment of intergenerational
> education is the conversation between the old a few
> years from death and the young a few years from
> birth.[20]

He speaks of the mutuality of "lifewide" (rather than life-
long) education, a continuum of learning wider than any
classroom. Fortunately there are real advances in intergenerational education as well as intergenerational childcare. Coles'
children also envision the elderly in their reflections on life's
purpose. To the question "What about me matters most?" a
fifth grader responds, "I'm the one at home who can make
our Gramps laugh!"

Even those in so-called aging parishes, and other communities without significant young-family populations, can learn to
respond with co-feeling as advocates and care-givers for "other
people's children." The call to interdependence and responsiveness modeled in the Incarnation is ageless. If we hope to
create a purposeful future, we have much to learn from envisioning childhood. Children remind us of the need to make
faithful choices about the present with an eye to the future.

Reflecting on children's lives also starts us thinking about
growth, maturity, aging, and God's identification with the
whole of humanity. Robert Coles, I recently learned, is now
interested in interviewing elderly persons. George Eliot in
Middlemarch confirmed this connection between childhood
and age a long time ago:

> Every limit is a beginning as well as an ending. Who
> can quit young lives after being in long company with
> them, and not desire to know what befell them in
> their after years.

Children point us toward God's promised reign. Elders, when they are seen in light of the Incarnation, confirm this ongoing promise.

Endnotes

1. Nancy L. and Robert N. Roth, eds., *We Sing of God: A Hymnal for Children* (New York: The Church Hymnal Corporation, 1989), p. 2.

2. See Richard Louv, *Childhood's Future* (Boston: Houghton Mifflin, 1991); Alex Kotlowitz, *There Are No Children Here: The Story of Two Boys Growing Up in the Other America* (New York: Doubleday, 1991); Philip Greven, *Spare the Child: The Religious Roots of Punishment and the Psychological Impact of Physical Abuse* (New York: Alfred A. Knopf, 1991).

3. Robert Coles, *The Moral Life of Children* (Boston: Houghton Mifflin, 1986), p. 15; see also p. 17.

4. The best published resource I've found for recent information on children and their families is a collection of studies edited by Frank Macchiarola and Alan Gartner, *Caring for America's Children* (Academy of Political Science, Vol. 37, No. 2, 1989), see pp. 145-46.

5. *Caring for America's Children*, p. 58.

6. This information is from a recent educational resource for parents, educators and parishes, "Family Violence and Abuse," A Policy Statement of the National Council of the Church of Christ, adopted November 14, 1990.

7. *Caring for America's Children*, p. 27.

8. This excellent guide—which emphasizes action based on prayer, Bible study, and assessment of parish and local community needs—was prepared by Kathleen A. Guy in cooperation with major Christian denominations and published in 1991. It is available from the Children's Defense Fund.

9. Robert Coles, *The Spiritual Life of Children* (Boston: Houghton Mifflin, 1990), p. 41.

10. *Ibid.*, p. 310.

11. Gabriel Moran, *Religious Education Development: Images for the Future* (Minneapolis: Winston Press, 1983), p. 198 and p. 176; see also his *Religious Education as a Second Language* (Birmingham, AL: Religious Education Press, 1989).

12. A good paperback introduction to this work in child development is *Mapping the Moral Domain: A Contribution of Women's Thinking to Psychological Theory and Education*, edited by Carol Gilligan, Janie Victoria Ward, and Jill McLean Taylor for the Center for the Study of Gender, Educa-

tion and Human Development (Cambridge, MA: Harvard University Press, 1988), p. xii.

13. *Ibid.*, pp. 122-23.

14. Coles, *Spiritual Life*, pp. 178-80.

15. Robert Coles, *The Political Life of Children* (Boston: Houghton Mifflin, 1986), p. 310.

16. Coles, *Spiritual Life*, p. 290.

17. *Ibid.*, p. 135.

18. John A. Bruce, "Children in an Adult World: The Roles of Spirit, Attitudes, and Expectations as Determinants of Wellness in Children," *Anglican Theological Review*, LXIII, No. 1 (Winter 1981), 45-46.

19. Leonel L. Mitchell, "The Communion of Infants and Little Children," *Anglican Theological Review*, LXXI, No. 1 (Winter 1989), 63-78.

20. *Religious Education as a Second Language*, pp. 234 and 236.

3

Grow Old Along with Me

Aging in Incarnational Perspective

Confession, they say, is good for the soul. I admit right away to some trepidation in speaking of elders because there are a whole batch of older adults, beloved relatives, and sage friends looking metaphorically over my shoulder as I write this chapter. They want me—and some even trust me—to tell their story accurately, "like it is." So from the first let me say that if you have a chance to spend time talking with older persons, go for it! In these days of hype and glitz, there is no substitute for plain speaking.

Conversation with friends is an ageless pleasure. As with all of us, older folk are the best tellers of their own stories. My wish is not to duplicate the art of their storytelling, but rather to present a picture gallery that is rich and diverse. This larger panorama will, I trust, evoke strong personal memories and images of your own. This is why I include stories of older adults who have been and remain a part of my identity and integrity, and I encourage you to invite your own companions along. Larger meanings and subtle truths about aging become more apparent when memories and personal stories take on flesh. Through the Incarnation God partakes in the fullness of human life, so we too must savor life's range to glimpse the fullness of God's incarnating gift to us.

I choose to start viewing aging "at home." My family, I have always thought, is eccentric and certainly not "typical." The older adults in my life are not diminished figures; indeed, they are larger-than-life, active, and curious teachers, critics, and friends who are inclined to do things in their own way, despite attempts of younger folk to tell them "just what to do"! Why, I wonder, are many people freer about giving advice to elders than to peers? Not I. Perhaps this is because my paternal grandmother did not take readily to advice. Wilhemina Ziegler, secretly called "Kaiser Bill" within the family circle, was feisty and fascinating. Asian youths, it is said, dream of the pleasures of being old not because their youth is not pleasant but because they do not fear the future. "Bill"—as you might suspect—was not Asian, yet she lived life, every bit of it, fearlessly. Now I wonder, was she really all that "eccentric" or did I simply expect "normal" elder behavior to be marked by passivity and stagnation? How could I have fallen for a stereotype like that when it runs contrary both to my experience and to my theological inheritance? Perhaps older adults are generally much more active and interesting characters than current stereotypes would lead us to believe.

And what of the Incarnation? Does the dignity and potential it promises for men and women fade with advancing years? Do we expect its empowering vision to dim beyond childhood's innocence? Here then is a second confession. It is very difficult not to fall prey to the negative assessments, whether subtle or blatant, this culture typically makes of older and aged adults. Unexamined warrants, conventional expectations, seemingly benign theories of human development, statistical tables about the end of life—all these can have a way of shaping as well as negating, if we are not careful, our closest personal experiences. Most of us, for example, approach the prospect of our own aging with touches of self-deception and denial, for "ageism" is above all an attitudinal sin deeply embedded in cultural soil. It is so often taken for granted that we might tend to ignore the harm it does.

The word "ageism" was first coined by Robert Butler in his 1968 study *Why Survive? Being Old in America*, and a classic, unguarded statement of "ageism" is found in Simone de Beauvoir's *The Coming of Age*: "The vast majority of mankind looks upon the coming of old age with sorrow or rebellion, and it fills them with more aversion than death itself." But ageism existed long before we had a name for it; Shakespeare showed a bias against age when he wrote, "Age, I do abhor thee, youth, I do adore thee." At the end of the nineteenth century English statesman Benjamin Disraeli—unlike our late, great statesman of aging, Senator Clyde Pepper—was downright hostile in asserting, "Almost everything that is great has been done by youth." The negative assessment of old age is not only a recent habit. Thomas Cole's new study, *The Journey of Life: A Cultural History of Aging in America*, traces the evolution of distinct historical perspectives and stereotypes. This country's consciousness of aging as a distinct social reality began in the mid to late nineteenth century, about the same time pediatrics was established as a medical specialty. Today Cole describes the creation of a "professional industry" largely preoccupied with solving the "scientific problem" of aging; he encourages us to return instead to ancient perspectives on aging as a "moral and spiritual frontier."[1]

Of course, many of us today would protest we are not "ageist" and rush to join in refiguring aging in glowing terms. Yet superficial optimism is no answer to false pessimism. The fact that we have to protest against stated social norms in order to redraft more realistic images suggests we are dealing with a complex, pervasive social pattern. Nostalgia for elderly people we used to know, encomiums for "outstanding" (read exceptional) elderly persons, and occasional compassionate outcries can only sentimentalize what is in fact a situation of widespread social sinfulness, and a theological error as well.

Here is a third and still another confession. Christian churches have not on the whole promoted healthy perspectives and futures for older adults. As we will see, despite the biblical record to the contrary, among people of the Good News the overall impression is that growing older is indeed "bad news." Churches have tended to view older adults as passive recipients of care and services, emphasizing ministry *to* their older members rather than supporting ministry *by* them. One of the most influential of all Christian theologians, St. Augustine, describes old age as "an inferior age, lacking in lustre, weak and more subject to disease." He concludes with perspicacity, "And it leads to death."

Modern theologians have generally reinforced these negative patterns of meaning as well. The underlying disdain for aging among people of faith has led an astute contemporary critic, Constance Buchanan, to charge Jewish and Christian theologians with promoting "theological ageism." She observes that many theologies of aging begin with the unexamined presupposition that aging is inevitably marked by a series of losses. Such negativity belies a deeper cultural problem.

> The question of aging...must be understood as one that itself raises even more fundamental questions about prevailing conceptions in American religion and society of human being and the human life cycle....primarily in relation to two norms: the location of fulfillment in the peak of mid-life and of its meaning in independence and power....That this experience is *not* the human norm can be illustrated by

examining at least one other kind of experience in American society, that of women.[2]

As long as theologians and preachers uncritically promote independence in mature males as the model for all human beings, we will be unable to address ageism successfully in our churches.

My central point—one to which we shall return in later chapters on work and on intimacy—is that when positive human value is ascribed to a "peak" of assertive, independent activity achieved at mid-life, then any growth beyond this point is perceived as inevitable decline regardless of anything theologians might say about the goodness of human life in its entirety. This model is graphically called the "peak/slope" model of human development. Attitudes toward aging are unavoidably and intrinsically caught up in our views of what is "normal" and "desirable" for human life, yet the blunt truth is that all, and not just some, of our best friends are aging. Who among us is getting any younger? Are we all then headed for yet another "fall," this time down the slippery slope of human development? Could this be God's plan?

Seeing aging in the light of God's incarnating presence suggests other alternatives and leads to thinking about the meaning of life in its totality. By focusing on older adults, much as I tried to illuminate theology with the lives of children, I hope to explore not only what it is to be human, but also to *stay* human. I am not going to argue that aging is loss any more that I am going to insist that aging is wonderful; as you might suspect, I prefer to think of "Christ in us and we in Christ," and say that aging is continuing incarnation. The truth of the story of God's incarnation is ageless. This is the implicit standard of a God who rejoices and joins in the whole of creation, and whose presence is fully "re-presented" in every stage of life or else in none.

Incarnational perspectives on childhood reveal and recast the attitudes we have about assuming power over the lives of others. So, too, does theological reflection on aging challenge

63

American cultural assumptions about unconditioned human autonomy and freedom. Where do older people fit into the social scheme of things? How is God's incarnating presence apparent in old age? What is the meaning of loss at any age? Is independence the sole standard for success and the central measure of identity? Are there limits to growth as a human being and growth toward God? Just when does growth stop?

"Youth Shows But Half"

I went to the Bible in search of narratives about aging, but frankly I did not expect to find stories with images as full as those of Matthew's gospel's visions of childhood. Wrong again. Inspired by a desire to be reintroduced to the Bible's elder citizens, I learned to read even the most familiar biblical passages with keener vision, and I recommend this journey of discovery to you. For example, I discovered for the first time an intergenerational triptych in Luke, which of course had been there all along. In Luke's infancy narrative, the story of the child Jesus' presentation in the Temple is surrounded and supported by two strong pious elders. As Jesus and his family enter the Temple they are welcomed by the devout and religious Simeon, who realizes that this child is the glory of Israel. In a song that has been prayed through the centuries in Western liturgies, the *Nunc Dimittis*, he proclaims, "These eyes of mine have seen the Savior, whom you have prepared for all the world to see." Then the eighty-four-year-old prophet and widow Anna emerges from Temple confines where she has spent most of her life in prayer and fasting. This aged widow is the one chosen to interpret the meaning of the event to others gathered about the Temple:

> At that moment [Anna] came [forth from the Temple], and began to praise God and to speak about the child to all who were looking for the redemption of Jerusalem. (Lk. 2: 38)

64

It is too bad we don't have Anna's song of praise to sing as well, though I can imagine it would have caused the prophet Isaiah to smile with familiarity. Separately and together Anna and Simeon recognize the incarnate one, the Child whose presence heralds a new age.

Anna breaks other molds. She is a prophet, one of a few aged women named in the biblical record whose worth is independent of her ability to provide offspring. Together Simeon's and Anna's greatness lies not only in their strong piety, but also in their openness to perceiving God's will anew and announcing God's purpose for humanity. They are both guardians of ancient wisdom and bearers of the new creation. Notice these elders did not say, "We've never done it this way before." Instead, old people in Luke, as biblical scholar John Koenig notes, are "visionaries, futurists... [who] exercise a prophetic ministry which enables young people to see the 'big picture' of God's plan."[3] Emma Lou Benignus also observes that when God wants "significant change," older adults are often the ones who bring the summons. Perhaps elders are chosen to seek a newer world because they have lived long enough to discern between novelties and a larger purpose. Their sense of time, at least their lived awareness of it, takes on a new perspective. Jeanette Piccard, ordained as an Episcopal priest when she was seventy-nine, believed a true luxury of old age is being able to see more of the narrative as a whole.

Anna and Simeon are not alone among elderly biblical trailblazers and adventurers. Moses' significance for the Israelites began when he was eighty; Paul was sixty when he planned a new ministry in Spain. There are countless others: Enoch, Jacob, Abraham and Sarah, Elizabeth and Zechariah. Several of these stories also emphasize the interrelation of children and elders, pointing to the ways children are enriched in their encounters with old people. If children are incarnate "signs" of God's reign, surely many of the Bible's older prophets are enfleshed "heralds" of the new. Could it be that older adults in the Bible are not primarily objects *for* ministry, but spiritual agents who from the perspective of their age have vital ministries to offer the young as well as their contemporaries? Elders in the Bible are authorities on tradition and current affairs, and great things are still anticipated from them. They show us that at any age we are blessed and empowered through God's incarnating presence to play a part in transforming the world.

The modern psychologist of human development Erik Erikson names this spiritual gift "generativity." By that he means older adults' spiritual capacity to express deep concern not simply for themselves, but for the welfare of future generations. To generativity Erikson adds the spiritual gift of integrity, finding in elders a longing for wholeness and coherence, a way of joining what they believe to how they live their lives. Erikson's description of generativity aligned with integrity is similar to the attribute of "co-feeling" found among adolescents, although the elderly's ethic of care is informed by a broader perspective and includes a larger sense of stewardship for the whole. A friend of mine in her late seventies who was once the elected leader of a Protestant denomination fits Erikson's category of generativity. When asked what she does with her days, she replies, "I am in the Justice and Liberation business." My friend remains a formidable and persuasive channel of God's grace. Generativity, like co-feeling, underscores a pattern of mutuality and identification of purpose modeled by the Incarnation. Far from denying them, God seems to depend on old people's abilities and contributions.

Eminent nineteenth-century poets confirm the Bible's incarnational expectation of transforming the world by becoming involved it in. I learned to love English poetry as a teenager; my favorite relative, Great-Auntie Ann, was responsible. Ann—whom I would now describe as a *typically* energetic, farseeing older adult—was still unique. Among her other accomplishments, Ann taught mathematics, read Latin and the classics, founded a women's collegiate honorary society named Mortar Board, and was the first woman to fly in Ohio!

One day when we were deep in conversation, she fussed about simplistic, "gooey" views of aging. I mentioned an all-time favorite tag line for "aging" found on many greeting cards: "Grow old along with me!" Ann mischievously insisted we find and read the original poem in its entirely. A far cry from the Hallmark sentimentality I expected, Robert Browning's "Rabbi Ben Ezra" is a complex, honest, feisty, and profound epic, well worth reading aloud and discussing with friends of any age. Here is the first stanza in full:

> Grow old along with me!
> The best is yet to be,
> The last of life, for which the first was made:
> Our times are in his hand
> Who said, "A whole I planned,
> Youth shows but half; trust God: see all, be not afraid!

Browning, who lived to be seventy-seven, concludes this intensely purposeful poem:

> So, take and use thy work:
> Amend what flaws may lurk,
> What strain o' the stuff, what warpings past the aim!
> My times be in thy hand!
> Perfect the cup as planned!
> Let age approve of youth and death complete the same!

Browning, it seems, knew about generativity long before Erikson called it a spiritual gift. Like Anna and Simeon, the aged rabbi expects to contribute to God's plan.

Another of my great-aunt's favorite poems was Alfred Lord Tennyson's "Ulysses." At first I was surprised that this landlocked midwesterner favored a seafarer's lament. Then we read the poem together, and I recall Ann intoning this poem's concluding lines:

> . . .you and I are old;
> Old age has yet his honor and his toil;
> Death closes all; but something ere the end,

Some work of noble note, may yet be done....

'Tis not too late to seek a newer world....

Tho' much is taken, much abides: and tho'
We are not now that strength which in old days
Moved earth and heaven; that which we are, we are:
One equal temper of heroic hearts,
Made weak by time and fate, but strong in will
To strive, to seek, to find, and not to yield.

My great-aunt and Tennyson both lived to be eighty-three. Each expressed older adults' longing to serve. Like Browning, Tennyson proclaims the purposiveness of elders, and his "Some work of noble note, may yet be done" parallels Browning's "So, take and use thy work."

Growing up to be old still involves *growing*. God's identification with humanity does not stop at the nativity creche; it continues to the cross and beyond to everlasting life. Moreover, God's plan unfolds not by glossing over "flaws" and "warps" but by realistic and straightforward noting of life's particularities. What we are, we are. Novelist May Sarton's book about a modern nursing home resident is aptly entitled *As We Are Now*. How many times have we tried to compliment older persons by remarking, "You don't look your age!" One advocate for aging expresses her weariness in being told that "the less I look like and act like my own age, the better I am!" Who, I wonder, is troubled most by aging? Most older adults do not deny reality; they have seen too much of it to lie about the present.

As we explore the incarnational dimensions of aging, there is no need for theological romanticism. Concrete reality, not abstraction, is the substance of incarnational theology. I am reminded of a treasured line of graffiti from a New York subway train: "Nostalgia isn't what it used to be!" Vivid pictures and enfleshed stories of all ages reveal the fullness of God's providence. The biblical promise of a "God with us" is not insurance against loss or grief, but a promise of presence throughout our lives. The prophet Isaiah recalls this covenant:

> Listen to me, House of Jacob,
> all you who remain of the House of Israel,
> you who have been carried since birth,
> whom I have carried since the time you were born.
>
> In your old age I shall be still the same,
> when your hair is grey, I shall still support you.
> I have already done so, I have carried you,
> I shall still support and deliver you.
> (Is. 46:3-4, Jerusalem Bible)

For those of us fortunate enough to live well into old age, youth is truly half.

"The Last of Life"

This last decade of the twentieth century has been styled by American contemporary observers as an "Age of Aging" and "The Long-Lived Society." Such new names for our aging society suggest various statistical descriptions and raise a blunt, preliminary inquiry: Who among us is "old"? What are the embodied realities of aging in America?

In looking at terminology it is important to remember older adults are not another "class," but represent an increasingly predictable stage of human development. Conversations about the aged are not about "them," but about our present or future selves; to paraphrase the cartoon character Pogo, "We have met the aging, and they are us." While there are many more than fifty-seven varieties of elderly persons, current demographic nomenclature divides the older population into three groups: the "young old," who are sixty-five to seventy-four, the "just plain old," who are seventy-five to eighty-four, and the "oldest old," who are eighty-five and older. Some of you with ageless curiosity may inquire about age limits for the category of the "oldest old." Shakespeare in *King Lear* gives the best description I've heard of the oldest among the "oldest old":

> O Sir! You are old;
> nature in you stands on the verge
> of her confine.

The Bard's image suggests another term from contemporary reports on aging. The "frail elderly" are found in all three groups, although they are particularly but not necessarily among the "oldest old." Perspective remains essential in combatting society's ageism. The American Association of Retired Persons (AARP) reports that ninety-four percent of all retired persons are "hale and hearty," not "feeble and frail." Moreover, despite gloomy assertions to the contrary, it is important to emphasize only five percent of the U. S. population over sixty-five is institutionalized at any one time. That is only twenty-two percent of adults aged eighty-five or more, which means that seventy-eight percent of the "oldest old" are out and about.

Why then does media and other journalistic coverage of "the elderly" repeatedly focus on those living in what I used to call "old folks' homes"? The unvarnished truth is that most older persons simply live "at home." Earlier we noted that Anglican theology is contextually clearest when it comes "home," and we should turn our assumptions about aging homeward. Geographically most elders stay put. Many older adults live on their own; half of all women over sixty-five live alone, as do fourteen percent of elderly men; the remaining live with relatives or with a spouse. Families in America, not residential institutions, are the main givers of personal care and help to elderly in need. Friends and families provide what one gerontologist calls a "social care system." With this image in mind we should caution against viewing living alone negatively. Interdependent contact with others is important. With support from family, friends, and neighbors, many elderly citizens living "home alone" are far from lonely.

Since patterns of institutionalization are relatively low, what has changed in American society to make many of us more conscious, if not fearful, of aging and of the elderly? Why do many Christians today seem to set aside the Incarnation's affirmation of God's in-dwelling presence among all of God's children, including the "oldest old"? For one thing, there have been dramatic population shifts involving the elderly. At the time of Jesus only one in ten of his contemporaries lived to be fifty. Today we have moved from an average life expectancy of forty-seven at the beginning of this century to the present average figure of seventy-five years. Other factors, of course, affect longevity. Recent life expectancy rates for men are 71 years, compared to 78.3 for women; for Caucasians the figure is 75.2, set against the low figure of 69.6 for African Americans. Among eighty-year-olds there are one hundred women for every forty men. *The Wall Street Journal* recently reported that the United States is approaching a maximum longevity of eighty-five.

To add a note of historical perspective, the average life span during the sixteenth century at the time of the English Reformation's first Book of Common Prayer was about twenty-seven years. These days we have a lot more of life to pray for. With current increases in longevity patterns, elders' share of the total U.S. population has grown steadily. The percentage of persons in the overall population who are sixty-five and older was about four percent in 1920, eight percent in 1950, and eleven percent by 1984. By 2030 we can expect this figure to double.[4]

Are you dizzy from reading so many statistics? Please hold on for just a few more. It is important to know about the particularities and contexts of older adults' lives in order to suggest theological perspectives that fully attend to their realities. Truly staggering statistics about older adults in the United States relate to quality-of-life issues. This country's total population of elderly persons is more sharply stratified into rich and poor than the younger members of society. Poverty is an increasingly distressing problem, especially for women and ethnic minorities. Women are only sixty percent of those sixty-five and older, but they make up seventy-two percent of the aged poor. Moreover, eighty percent of aged African American women and half of elderly women from Hispanic populations are poor. In short, poverty among America's elderly mirrors statistics found among our children. As several observers have noted, typically those who are old and poor were young and poor at another point in their lives. This intergenerational similarity is largely a question of gender and race. Even with additional complications of health and economic hardship, I was still shocked to learn that between one-quarter and one-third of all suicides in America are committed by people over sixty-five.

There is considerable debate these days about statistics and their meaning. Statistical estimates can not only be misleading, their definitiveness can also result in a wide variety of "absolute" interpretations that distract us from important root questions. By way of illustration, a friend of mine, Robert Browne, who is in the risky though biblically-inspired business of being a futurist, enjoys telling this story:

> A man was driving up a narrow mountain road. Suddenly a car came around the bend up ahead. It was speeding, heading for him on his side of the road. He swerved to avoid hitting it and, as the car passed, its driver leaned out the window and shouted, "PIG!"
>
> He felt more than a touch of anger until he drove around that bend and he hit a pig.
>
> You see, the word was out, but the meaning was not clear.

Today there are three key debates among politicians and policy-makers about the meaning of life in an aging society. For better and for worse, religion helps fashion cultural patterns of meaning. I outline these debates, so apparently "secular," to explore where there are openings and connections between contemporary attitudes toward aging and theological principles revealed in the Incarnation.

One debate focuses on how "well off" the elderly really are. There are groups on the right of the political spectrum, for example, who think elders are receiving too much support, and accuse them of draining off resources that America's children—and her middle-aged "baby boomers"—deserve. Some critics add that since many older adults do not contribute economically, they should not cause "social burdens" for younger citizens. In large measure this is a distracting debate. The Children's Defense Fund and the AARP agree that poor children tend to grow up to be poor adults. What *is* surprising is that there tends to be little secular or religious discussion in this country about the relationship of poverty and aging. The same can be said of children and poverty. Statistics on elderly poverty overlook the fact that not all of the risks of growing old are related to the aging process itself. The social construction of aging, like that of childhood, is in part dependent on how a society chooses to provide for those in need. This is an opening for bringing religious resources more to the forefront of the debate. We could begin by asking if poverty among older adults is inevitable from biblical and incarnational perspectives.

The impact of current policies on the treatment of America's elderly is clear in a second debate focusing on the health of older Americans. In raising the issue of illness, I do not want to suggest older Americans are by and large sickly. Three out of four deaths among elderly patients result from heart disease, cancer, or stroke, yet the probabilities of dying from these same three diseases at age sixty-five are not greatly different from those for newborn children.[5] Today's health debate is whether elderly persons are healthier now and therefore do not need extensive medical coverage. This is actually several debates rolled up into one question. The response is yes, if being healthy is equated with Americans living statistically longer than any other older generation in history, and no if we consider many elderly are not dying of diseases as they once did but are learning to live with them into "oldest age."

However, finding adequate short- and long-term medical care is identified by elders as both raising their greatest fears and involving the highest financial cost. For many older Americans income maintenance and health care financing are directly and often fearfully related. A relatively new factor addressed by researchers on aging is "illness-engendered poverty." This type of poverty results from Medicare and other policies requiring elderly persons to "spend down" to poverty levels before receiving coverage for long-term care. It can mark the beginning of a wider poverty spiral; consequences of this policy leave behind impoverished spouses and sometimes other dependents as well. Moreover, the cost of paying for a year or less of nursing home finances, at three or four thousand dollars a month, is sufficient to impoverish all but the most affluent families. The United States and the Republic of South Africa are the only two developed countries without a system of long-term care for elderly citizens.

It may be true Americans do not fear aging and frailty per se; instead, many dread the ways this culture provides for elderly in need. It is difficult to ask older adults to "fear not" and trust the God of Isaiah who "still supports and delivers" them, when realistically their society is not readily providing basic humane health care. From an incarnational perspective it is sinful to leave any child of God valueless, beyond assistance when in need. Humanity's continuing co-responsibility with God in Christ for bringing about God's reign escalates the issue of care for elderly persons beyond humanistic ideals to divine commands to "love one another as [Christ] loves us."

In other countries the emotional and spiritual landscape for aging can be different. I have, for example, a seventy-five-year-old aunt who lives alone in Canada. Aunt Alice's income is supported through a small, national "old age" pension, while her emotional and spiritual resources are large and rich. This energetic "spinster" is always up and about relating to a large circle of friends old and new. This tends to frustrate American family members who can seldom reach her at home by phone. Alice is usually out tending the garden and playing with her two wonderfully spoiled "doggies," as well as providing support and assistance to her "older" neighbors who, she notes, are "only" eighty-four and ninety-two.

My aunt much prefers to be on her own and is thankful she can care for herself and for others. Formal religion comes to her directly and frequently through television and radio programs. She speaks of the future without fear of penury, untended illness, or unnatural dependency. There will no doubt be other losses in the last of her life, but I believe she will approach these with her customary resourcefulness. Alice once told me that although she was raised in this country and lived here for most of her life, she could not imagine growing old in America.

Theology is truest when it is contextual, meeting us personally at home, and that brings me to the third complex debate about aging in America. How should we care for older adults who are not able to recognize whether they are indeed "at home"? Are those whose mental capacities are deranged by illness still vehicles of the Incarnation? So far in this chapter I have talked about the vast majority of elderly Americans who are in command of their mental powers. To be disabled at any age is cause for social stigma in America. In biblical times lepers were singled out for shunning; in this culture those with so-called mental illnesses are among the least understood and tolerated populations. When an older adult is unpredictable, violent, or nonsensical rather than obedient and quiet, ageism's prejudice is doubly intense. "Senility" simply means "old age," yet in popular usage it reinforces many negative stereotypes of the aged. Older adults, who are generally stoic about physical illness, admit to fearing "senility" most of all. Many of them assume that serious cognitive incapacity comes with aging, or mistakenly accept confusion among older people as a consequence of the aging process. There are older adults who experience loss of memory for hours or even days. Temporary memory loss—sometimes called "sundowner's syndrome"—is often a symptom of other diseases and calls for accurate diagnosis and prompt medical attention. Recently, however, Alzheimer's disease has revived fears of insanity among elders.

I want to focus for a moment on Alzheimer's because a group of older clergy recently suggested to me that for them it proves the limitations of incarnational theology. When I pressed them for further information, one curtly replied, "How could you possibly relate in a Christlike manner when your own mother does not recognize you?" When an older adult cannot communicate with us, and when that person's behavior toward loved ones is hostile or paranoid, is it possible to believe that Christ still dwells within? The deeper issues raised here touch upon what we believe is essential about being "human." My challengers seemed to assume that humanity was defined by relational, cognitive abilities, yet why should we assume Christ's presence is absent from victims of advanced Alzheimer's? How is this different from gazing upon a desperately ill premature infant, or a beloved friend in the last, long throes of death from AIDS?

Alzheimer's does raise poignant challenges to the persistent truth of incarnational theology. It is a progressive neurological disorder that leads gradually to complete cognitive loss and eventually death. Like cancer and AIDS, its social stigma is so strong that some family members and elders delay diagnosis, deny onset of the disease, or refuse to tell patients the truth of their condition. I have heard wildly inflated predictions about the frequency of Alzheimer's among elderly patients. It is true that with more accurate diagnosis of cognitive impairments, as well as a lengthening of the average life span, the number of Alzheimer's victims will increase. Its prevalence is now estimated at three percent among the "young old," eighteen percent for the "old," and for individuals over eighty-five the rate is close to forty-seven percent. As with AIDS and cancer, better education about the disease is also essential. A federal government report's guidelines for Alzheimer's treatment include instructions

> to *treat disability not abnormality*, to reverse associated curable illnesses, to limit troublesome symptoms, and to maintain continued support.[6]

With better diagnosis of Alzheimer's, and over 150 possible causes of confusion, we can now name and treat abnormal behaviors as illness-produced, rather than assuming old people are inevitably confused and crazy.

Neurologist Oliver Sacks, author of *Awakenings* and other studies of adults suffering from extreme neurological disorders, aptly describes perception and communication as the two key issues for family, friends, and professional caregivers. He encourages us to keep our perceptions of patients' inabilities open to new insight, acknowledging our assumptions and data may not be fully accurate. Sacks also challenges us not to define others' worth primarily by their abilities to communicate with us, and cautions against underestimating any ill person's struggle to maintain personal identity even with demential and delusional behaviors. Alzheimer's victims, for example, enjoy human companionship, giving and receiving love, long after they have lost the ability to talk clearly or to care for themselves. The ability to feel and respond to feelings remains.

In baptism we are "marked as Christ's own for ever." An "aging-is-continuing-incarnation" paradigm is everlasting; it prevails whether or not we recognize Christ within another. It pertains even when a member of the body of Christ can no longer fathom what this means. God does not forget us even though our memories fail; of this I am confident. Mother Teresa once described the poor of Calcutta as made in the image of Christ although they were living now "in such distressing disguise." The perceptual challenge of relating to victims of Alzheimer's and other confused persons is to honor their unexpected reality, to see through this "distressing disguise" to the child of God within.

I do not intend to underestimate the costs to relatives, friends, and other caregivers when intimacy, reciprocity, and cognitive skills are different or absent. Alzheimer's caregivers, whose efforts are in demand "thirty-six hours a day," often need assistance as well.[7] Incarnational theology is persistently contextual; its promises extend to all who struggle to grow in love toward one another. Although I do not have an elderly relative with Alzheimer's, I have witnessed a spouse at midlife experience his last demented days of life. The incarnational gift of everlasting life leaves no child of God valueless. The doctrine of the Incarnation invites us to experience theology intimately, including life's attendant losses and risks. This ideal is not an abstraction but an embodied expectation continuing throughout the last of life.

The church is supposed to have a special competency about the meaning of life, and perhaps this is one reason many older adults find particular merit in lives of faith, often becoming "more religious" in their latter days. Surveys indicate that the elderly are the most religious group in American society in terms of the influence religion has on their personal lives, their commitment to put religious beliefs to work, and the comfort and support they experience from religious activities.[8] This does not mean participation in church or synagogue services axiomatically increases with age; usually attendance is highest when people are in their sixties and slowly declines thereafter. Difficulty in hearing and other physical impairments, as well as the need for better transportation, are repeatedly named as reasons why. Elderly patterns of religious participation, however, remind us to pause and ask, "What kind of activity does a life of faith require?" Personal religious practices—Bible reading, prayer, and meditation, communing with a friend or with nature or both—are more likely to increase. Silence can be rich with communication and comfort. In her poem "On Aging," African American poet Maya Angelou whimsically cautions:

> When you see me sitting quietly,
> Like a sack left on the shelf,
> Don't think I need your chattering.
> I'm listening to myself.[9]

Beyond their own families, elderly persons are most likely to discover new friendships through participation in religious activities. Many churches and synagogues offer extended relational networks. These institutions, and not old folks' residences, have the most advantageous personal access to elderly adults. This access can be a precious opportunity not only for those in "the last of life" but for the spiritual benefit of all God's children.

"So Take and Use Thy Work"

Ethicists frequently underscore the urgency, the moral imperative, of putting understanding to use at any age, and I think the older adults of my acquaintance would also concur with the value of envisioning aging as a moral and spiritual frontier. For these adults aging is not the end of involvement in life, but often signifies the beginning of a different kind of involvement—one that acknowledges God's continuing presence. The particularities of aging suggest there may be distinct dimensions to a spirituality of aging. Of course there is no specific theology for older persons that differs markedly from everyone else's, yet the belief that elders have a distinctive spirituality to offer others is not new. In Navajo culture young people are sent to learn wisdom by spending time with elders, much as I was sent and drawn to spend time with my

Great-Auntie Ann. In fact ours is one of the few societies that does not value its elders for their possession of spiritual wisdom. This is our loss. What might a theology of aging inspired by incarnational insights and ideas look like? What would be its central characteristics? Perhaps such a theology would not simply be a tonic for the "oldest old" but would be good for the rest of us.

A theology derived from paying close attention to older adults would, first of all, *put memories to work*. Anglicans use a Greek word to describe this action in the eucharistic liturgy. *Anamnesis* refers to a poignant kind of remembering, which brings the past so powerfully into the present that a new future is able to be affirmed. When the people proclaim "Christ has died. Christ is Risen. Christ will come again," we are putting our memories to work. From the perspective of time and distance, memory allows us to discover the meaning of God's incarnating presence anew. Starting with the acknowledgment of our distinct inheritance, identity takes shape over time. Thus in the Jewish religion, Passover begins with a child asking an elder, "Why do we do these things?" W. Paul Jones, a Protestant theologian, writes with sensitivity to older adults' spiritual gifts:

> Remembering is a fundamental avocation of aging itself....What rare power comes in remembering the past so as now to accept it, forgive it, relive it, reconstitute it. This is transfiguration.[10]

Putting memories to work, whether in liturgies or daily life, can be a source of healing as well. Researchers, pastors, caregivers, and the elderly themselves are turning to a relatively new technique, drawn from family systems therapy, called "life review." In this process, also know as "reminiscence therapy," older adults are encouraged to reappropriate their memories either in a guided group setting or with an individual confidant.[11] The goal here is to turn from potentially negative introspection and brooding to increasing awareness of life's values and meanings. Elders are going to think about the past anyway. Putting memories to work breaks through denial and knots of unarticulated pain. This process can allow and deepen perspective, as well as open opportunity for forgiveness of others and eventually of one's self. Goethe wrote, "One only has to grow older to become more tolerant. I see no fault that I might not have committed myself," while the dying Beethoven observed, "We all make mistakes, everyone just makes different mistakes." Putting memory to work allows us literally to revisualize time, moving separated and separating incidents toward a vision of the larger picture. Memory is a source of generativity, illuminating God's presence in our lives as our own sense of understanding evolves over time.

Incarnational theology honors human life as a whole. Therefore another essential component in a theology of aging is the *fundamental appreciation of human embodiment.* Many of us do not easily or happily think about physical contact with and among older adults. This may be traced to our culture's distorted and narrow prescriptions for physical beauty, as well as to socially-constructed limitations on intimacy and sexuality. A newly-married grandmother told me her own children labeled her sexuality as "inappropriate, even disgusting." Yet we do not just *have* bodies, we *are* bodies. This awareness is underscored through Hebrew Scripture's emphasis on the goodness of God's creation, and the New Testament's focus on divine incarnation as "the Word became flesh and dwelt among us" (Jn. 1:14). For those who affirm God's continuing presence, the Word still becomes flesh.

A simple awareness of breathing, for example, can open up an experience of a God whose Spirit—literally, whose breath—travels over the waters (Gen. 1:2). At any age the experience of waking up each morning can leave us feeling lucky we can still breathe. In his poem "Grace," George Herbert writes:

And now in age I bud again,
After so many deaths I live and write:
I once more smell the dew and rain,
And relish versing: O, my only Light,
   It cannot be
   That I am he
On whom Thy tempests fell all night.

A realistic Christian theology of aging will take embodiment seriously. The "oldest old" agree. In a recent survey elderly persons in nursing homes were polled about daily concerns; their priorities focused on movement and touch. The first was the freedom to move about the residence and the second was the desire for regular contact with others. For many institutionalized elders, these are the central concerns about the quality of their lives. Did you know that forty percent of nursing home residents are placed in devices restricting movement? In several states there is now a legislative movement for "restraint-free care," which relies on miniature beepers to notify the staff of the residents' whereabouts. Meanwhile, I have a good friend whose ninety-six-year-old mother was known as the Great Liberator. Katharine could not only get out of her own restraints, she would travel the halls untying others.

Recent studies of older adults living outside as well as in residences emphasize the importance of friendship in maintaining emotional and physical health. Friendships are essential for encouraging two aspects of psychological growth: "intimacy," ongoing close contact with others, and "reciprocity," the ability to be supportive as well as to receive support. This suggests an incarnational model. Few elders want to be objects of care. They desire interdependent relationships in which they can appreciate one another's uniqueness and offer help as well.

Friendships for elders, as for us all, are a critical resource in coming to terms with change and loss. For those who have assumed traditional women's roles, widow-to-widow programs provide companions with similar backgrounds someone to talk with about daily events and past experiences. They are an effective way of building upon and contributing to older women's relational identity. Listening to elders and learning more about the rich variety of their friendships will help caregivers and policy-makers provide more humane support. Just being friendly means a lot. While fundamental appreciation of embodiment is a central component of incarnational theology in general, intimacy and reciprocity can be lifelines for elders.

In a similar vein, a theology of aging needs to *convey realistic perspectives about both life and God.* There is little in life older persons have not experienced, and it is important to grant them the dignity of not denying what they know from their own experience to be true. If they are enduring suffering, this needs to be named and not wished away. Negative aspects of life at any age should not be denied or minimized. The challenge is to bring theological reflection into proximity with peoples' lives, to honor their reality, whether or not it is unexpected or different from our own.

Read, for example, the new edition of Malcolm Boyd's prayers, *Are You Running With Me, Jesus?* It is full of direct, familiar images, real prayers about the highs and lows of life, including those experienced by persons in a retirement home. Boyd's meditations confirm that most elders prefer plain speaking to sententiousness. When ninety-six-year-old Katharine broke her hip and was feeling poorly, her priest asked if she would like a prayer before he left. "Yes," she replied, "but you'd better make it a good one!"

Many elders possess a theology full enough to encompass a sense of God's absence as well as presence. The psalms are favored texts for many among the "oldest old." I know a scholar of Hebrew Scripture who complains that modern liturgical editions of the Psalter have removed, cleaned up, or tamed down the psalms' "laments," their outcries against human suffering and God's seemingly on-again-off-again response that includes absence, silence, and abandonment. It is important to honor what mystics throughout the ages have known, and what elders today can still teach us, about discerning God's apparent presence *and* absence at moments in our lives. A theology with grounded, realistic perspectives about both God and life recognizes the incarnate fullness of the human condition and its profound sense of struggling with God.

Such realistic perspectives can also lead us and our loved ones to ask questions and make preparations not only for death, but for the process of dying itself. Many elders are voicing their fears of hard, sterile, and needlessly prolonged dying at the hands of modern medicine. Answers and conclusions do not come easily, since medical technology has seemingly outpaced old cultural expectations about a "natural" death. We are faced with new technologically-assisted situations that may look like "life" but are not. Indeed, medical communities are redefining "death" itself. A realistic theology of aging leads us to ask more, not fewer, hard questions about the quality of life and the process of dying. New definitions of death require religious professionals as well as other Christians to develop new moral understandings, vocabulary and guidelines about the end of life. Writing a living will or naming a proxy for health care decisions are but two of the legal aids that are increasingly utilized. In *Surviving Death: A Practical Guide*, Charles Meyers, an Anglican priest and hospital administrator, helpfully interweaves information about medical technology alongside theological and moral perspectives, questions, and directions. Meyers hears and draws our attention to contemporary "laments" of human suffering. Here too spiritual perspectives on aging prove ageless, as they are clearly instructive for others faced with decisions about death and dying.

Incarnational theology is patterned on notions of a continuing relationship with God, of responsible struggle, and of taking hold of every bit of life. A theology of aging inspired by incarnational principles *underscores continuing interde-pendence with God.* In this regard classical Anglican theology is distinct from more reformed perspectives. The persistent sense of mutuality and continuing responsibility called for in the sacraments of baptism and eucharist go against the grain of "theologies for elders" that typically recommend total dependence on God. Such theologies derive from a model of aging as loss; giving up is expected. Passively accepting a "whatever-will-be-will-be" attitude can breed irresponsibility and apathy at any age. Among the frailest elderly, moreover, resignation can cause premature memory loss and depression, and it can hasten death. A theology of dependence for older adults is as misguided as a theology of autonomy for those at mid-life. A sound theology of interdependence does acknowledge aspects of dependence, including knowing the limits of self-sufficiency, making a healthy assessment of real losses, and recognizing finitude. It honors older adults' desires to relate and to contribute as well.

Incarnational perspectives on aging *reveal the persistently intrinsic value of human life.* Seeing the "oldest old," not just newborns, in the bright light of the Incarnation respects their inherent dignity. This is more than a humanistic perspective; it is a theological affirmation of the value of life created in God's image. Emphasis on the value of "being" suggests more of an Eastern spiritual orientation, a helpful corrective to this culture's love affair with "doing" all day long. This theological formation challenges the notion that women and men are only valuable when they produce children or make things. Paying attention to the spiritual wisdom of elders can free us from believing in frenetic activity as the measure of life. Life from an incarnational perspective is not valued solely for its activity, but for its essence.

From a Christian perspective transformation, and not degeneration, is at the core of life's meaning. As a former musician, I have treasured for years cellist Pablo Casals' description of his routine at age ninety-three:

For the past eighty years I have started each day in the same manner. It is not a mechanical routine but something essential to my daily life. I go to the piano, and I play two preludes and fugues of Bach. I cannot think of doing otherwise. It is a sort of benediction on the house. But that is not its only meaning for me. It is a rediscovery of the world of which I have the joy of being a part. It fills me with awareness of the wonder of life, with a feeling of the incredible marvel of being human.

Recently a retired clergyman, now an advocate of long bike trips, reminded me of the bicyclists' perception of the "peak/slope" phenomenon: "When you're over the hill, you pick up speed down the other side." The value of life is more than personal; it points us toward the generosity of the giver and the gift.

Older persons acknowledge God's continuing presence in a myriad of ways. One of these is the *ability to admit God as a confidant.* Theologians and gerontologists alike observe older adults developing deep personal bonds with God. Citing Matthew 28:20, "I am with you always, to the close of the age," theologian W. Paul Jones suggests the Incarnation refers to a relationship of "confidants." It is no wonder monks of all ages were traditionally given the name "old man," because as religious they were perceived to be closer to the truth of God's eternity. Interiority is a component of many older persons' religious experience. Emma Lou Benignus names skill in prayer as one of the gifts often given to older adults. She recommends spiritual reading in great mystics like Tauler, Teresa of Avila, and John of the Cross, and I would add Mechtild of Magdeburg, all of whom tell of a friendship with God marked by a depth of interiority and a familiarity possible through the perspective of time. "Real prayer or meditation," Malcolm Boyd writes, "is not so much talking to God as just sharing God's presence."

In my parish, there is a prayer circle formed by elders with profoundly patient intercessory powers. One day, as I fretting about a colleague who was ill, a member this circle in her nineties gently confided, "There, there, don't worry, we've *plenty* of time to pray for him." Like other elders of my acquaintance, she offers wisdom matured in companionship with God.

Finally, a proper theology of aging has *a sense of humor.* Humor is often born of long-lived perspective, an awareness of contradictions and absurdities in life's circumstance. Come to think of it, jokes are part of my family's lore about Grandmother Bill. We still giggle about her habit of writing the letters TM on top of all her pies. Bill would wait for an unsuspecting guest to ask what this stood for. She would attentively reply, "One means 'Tis Mince' and the other means 'T'ain't Mince.'" Laughter is often found in those stories we choose to name as part of our identity, our inheritance. Humor is a gift throughout journey, an imaginative response to life's incarnate contingencies. Phyllis Clay, an Alzheimer's caregiver, tells of her mother's ability to find humor in the most frustrating times:

> One day I was yelling at her because she had misplaced MY credit card just before we were...to go on a trip. She started to cry and said, "Oh, honey, I don't know what's the matter with me; sometimes I think I only have one marble left." We held each other and laughed and cried.[12]

Mark Twain wrote, "Wrinkles should merely indicate where smiles have been." Laughter is a natural component of a spirituality of aging.

As people of the Incarnation we enjoy, if we choose, the capacity for an infinite relationship with God. Envisioning aging in incarnational perspective, growing old in the knowledge of God's continuing manifestation and presence, challenges us to accept and reconsider normative assumptions about human life. I've suggested a spirituality illumined by the lives of older adults includes, at least, these seven dimensions:

putting memories to work
affirming embodiment
conveying realistic perspectives about life and death
underscoring interdependence with God
honoring the intrinsic value of human life
admitting God as a confidant, and
expressing humor.

This is a welcome theological tonic for all ages. Its characteristics are strong, personal, blunt, intimate, and restful. It encourages us to accept loss and growth alike throughout our lives, and affirms a moderate sense of autonomy. We don't have to look at the lessons elders have to teach us in isolation from the other generations in the life cycle. I invite you to "take and use" the work of elders. In effect, the question of aging also presses us to raise fundamental questions about the ways we work and play throughout the rest of our lives.

Endnotes

1. Thomas Cole, *The Journey of Life: A Cultural History of Aging in America* (Cambridge: Cambridge University Press, 1992).

2. Constance H. Buchanan, "The Fall of Icarus: Gender, Religion, and the Aging Society," in *Shaping New Vision: Gender and Values in American Culture,* Clarissa W. Atkinson, Constance H. Buchanan, and Margaret R. Miles, eds., *Studies in Religion,* No. 5 (Ann Arbor: U.M.I. Research Press, 1987), pp. 181-82.

3. Quoted in Emma Lou Benignus in "Challenge to Ministry: Opportunities for Older Persons," *Affirmative Aging* (Minneapolis: Winston Press, 1985), pp. 31-32.

4. The estimate for 2030 is 21%; see Jacob S. Siegel and Cynthia M. Taeuber, "Demographic Perspectives on the Long-Lived Society," *Daedalus,* "The Aging Society," Vol. 115, No. 1 (Winter 1986), 79.

5. Siegel and Taeuber, "Demographic Perspectives," p. 97; causes of death in the U.S. for elderly persons are: 44% from heart disease, 22% from cancer,

and 12% from stroke; for newborns the rates of eventual death are 41% from heart disease, 19% from cancer, and 10% from cerebrovascular disease.

6. U.S. Congress, Office of Technology Assessment, *Losing a Million Minds: Confronting the Tragedy of Alzheimer's Disease and Other Dementias* (Washington, DC: U.S. Government Printing Office, April 1987), p. 110. See also Denis A. Evans, *et alia*, "Prevalence of Alzheimer's Disease in a Community Population of Older Persons: Higher than Previously Reported," *Journal of the American Medical Association*, Vol. 262, No. 18 (Nov. 10, 1989), 2551.

7. Rosemary Bileszner and Peggy A. Shifflett, "The Effects of Alzheimer's Disease on Close Relationships Between Patients and Caregivers, *Family Relations*, Vol. 39, No. 1, 57-62.

8. Tex Sample, "The Elderly Poor, the Future and the Church," in David E. Oliver, ed., *New Directions in Religion and Aging* (New York and London: The Haworth Press, 1987), p. 134.

9. Maya Angelou, *And Still I Rise* (New York: Random House, 1978), p. 48.

10. W. Paul Jones, "Aging as a Spiritualizing Process," *Journal of Religion & Aging*, Vol. 1, No. 1 (Fall 1984), 6; in this description of a theology of aging I am particularly indebted to Jones. See also K. Brynolf Lyon, *Toward a Practical Theology of Aging* (Philadelphia: Fortress Press, 1985).

11. On this process see, for example, James W. Magee, "Life Review: A Spiritual Way for Older Adults," *Journal of Religion & Aging*, Vol. 3, Nos. 3/4 (Spring/Summer 1987), 23-33.

12. Phyllis L. Clay, "A Journey into Alzheimer's: A Personal Account," *Creative Change*, Vol. 11, No. 2 (Fall 1990), 9.

4

Making a Living

Incarnational Reflections on Work

recent movie, *The Gods Must Be Crazy*, depicts the trials and travails of a Kalahari bushman faced suddenly with modern culture in the form of a Coca-Cola bottle. This film's humor plays the working values and everyday knowledge of the gentle bushman against the bumbling modernity of more "civilized" Africans. Throughout this comedy the industrial and commercial symbol of the Coke bottle rings changes on the value and meaning of work in diverse cultural contexts. It is good fun to laugh at everyday assumptions, products, dress codes, and rules of etiquette, especially when these things we take for granted are viewed through the eyes of another culture. Yet humor, in its truthfulness, can expose deep terrain for future reflection and vast gulfs worthy of critical, theological reflection.

Work is a commonplace reality at the heart of daily living. It is such an ordinary expectation that we take it for granted and seldom stop to address the deeper significance of labor and its produce. Work is a profoundly ambiguous topic; through it we have both blessed and cursed each other. Studs Terkel, a popular author and vernacular observer of American laborers, in the book *Working* concludes that work "by its very nature [is] about violence, to the spirit as well as the body." While Shakespeare observed in *As You Like It* "How full of briars is this working-day world," early English reformer Richard Taverner, who wrote popular proverbs in the 1530s at the time English Bibles were first published, gave work a realistic, mixed review: "Labors once done, be sweet."

A basic definition might help. My Webster's dictionary defines "work" as "mental or physical labor in order to achieve something," and I am pleased to see thought as well as muscle implied in this description. As a scholar, I have long been fond of a line from Percy Dearmer's hymn text, "Thank we those who toiled in thought, many diverse scrolls completing." The dictionary's emphasis on intentionality seems apt as well. Work makes a difference in our lives; whether paid or not, full- or part-time, how we keep and sustain life is purposeful. Often the term "vocation" is used to underline the purposeful and permanent nature of each individual's work. Actually most people today engage in more than one occupation over a lifetime; thus "work," as most women know, is best seen as a plural noun. Whatever the combination of thought, skill, and physical strength, "work" primarily signifies regular engagements and occupations. I will employ this broad, foundational definition of work instead of the narrower classical economists' view of work, and its derivative, "working persons," which is defined in Adam Smith's terms as "labor that has an exchange value on the market."

I have rejected the more limited view of labor as "work for hire" because it plays havoc with the reality of human lives.

For example, many if not most of the world's citizens labor daily for sheer survival without a paid wage. My preference for a wider vision of work that includes all daily occupations—gathering or planting food, drawing water, collecting fuel for a fire, caring for children, and keeping house—is based on the theological affirmation of all God's people. Truthfully there are few among us of voting age and sound health who are not "working persons."

This definition invites further questions. "What are," the old Geneva catechism asked in its traditional language, "the ends of man?" What is the central work we are given to do? How do the fruits of labor reflect who we are as individuals and as members of a larger culture? In terms of our identity as modern-day Christians, what is the relation between "being" and "doing"? And what about the nature of the work we do: are some jobs more godly than others? A traditional inquiry for Protestants focuses on the salvific power of the work we do: does work reveal our faithfulness and justify our lives? From a developmental point of view, with its "peak/slope" assumptions, our working years are our best years and the fullest measure of maturity. But we might ask: does what we *do* as workers define who we truly *are* at our best?

Clearly, work makes a difference in our lives not only individually but corporately. English author and theologian Dorothy Sayers had the social dimensions of labor in mind when she asked, "Why work?" There is a wide variety of possible responses to Sayers' blunt inquiry. George Eliot noted, "The stomach sets us to work." Furthermore, there is a strongly assumed collective meaning to labor. Simply stated, subsistence work tells us what is necessary for life, and additional productivity reveals cultural values. As illustrated in *The Gods Must Be Crazy*, how we labor together signifies the way our society shapes and organizes itself, from the services and products needed for survival to those desired for living more abundantly. The perceptive nineteenth-century social critic John Ruskin, writing amid the full flush of England's industrialization, addressed the social implications of work forthrightly in *Sesame and Lilies*:

> Which of us...is to do the hard and dirty work for the rest—and for what pay? Who is to do the pleasant and clean work, and for what pay?

The social and occupational diversity of work, Ruskin concluded in *The Crown of Wild Olive*, is a communal reality:

> There must be work done by the arms, or none of us could live. There must be work done by the brains, or the life we get would not be worth having.

Individually and socially, work is a profoundly complex, ambiguous, and revealing topic.

It is surprising that modern theologians have not paid more attention to the working contexts of human lives as primary constructive grounds for theological reflection and formation. It occurs to me that one of the reasons clergy and other religious leaders flounder and usually flop in repeated attempts to get church members to define lay ministry is that these same leaders fail to address and grapple with everyday realities and questions relating to the work lives of lay people. Theology's neglect of work is particularly odd, given this society's increasing preoccupation with work in general and with the problems associated with work for hire: unemployment, underemployment, overwork, and self-definition only through work. In this chapter I intend to address this omission in part by exploring the topic of work as a contemporary area for Christian theological reflection. In particular I want to posit and affirm a belief about modern labor that comes out of nineteenth and early twentieth century Anglican theology. Simply stated, the Incarnation provides a means for interpreting the daily life of workers in the fullness of both material and spiritual values. This is a resource for helping us affirm and understand the link between faith and work. Specifically, the Incarnation offers a traditional theological vehicle for understanding who we are as "workers" in the broad, mature middle years of our lives.

There are several components to this inquiry. First of all, I will identify several significant biblical perspectives on work and workers. Second, I will point to some major strands within Anglican theology that address both workers and the public social ordering of work. What are distinctive Anglican perspectives on work and how does incarnational theology provide a lens for viewing and refreshing our insights about work? How do Anglican theologies of work differ from other theologies? Third, as an aid to theological reflection, I will sketch the central characteristics and assumptions about workers and the workplace in the United States. Part of becoming reacquainted with the diverse and changing world of work today involves not only learning from the reflections of sociologists and economists, but also hearing the voices of workers who labor in diverse occupations. These voices can turn us toward more concrete and realistic theological reflection and action in support of "making a living."

"Christ the Worker"

In *The Gods Must Be Crazy*, laboring villagers sing a song originally from Ghana. This spirited work song, whose English title is "Christ the Worker," uses repeated phrases to set a rhythm for performing repetitive labor such as hammering, and several of its verses suggest incarnational perspectives on work:

> Christ the worker,
> Christ the worker,
> born in Bethlehem,
> born to work and die for every one.
>
> ...Skillful craftsman,
> skillful craftsman,
> blessed carpenter,
> praising God by labor at his bench.

Heavy laden,
heavy laden,
gladly come to him,
he will ease your load and give you rest.

Christ the worker,
Christ the worker,
Love alive for us,
teach us how to do all work for God.[1]

The incarnate Christ here represents both the work of salvation and the labor of our hands. The depiction of Jesus as a craftsman—a "carpenter praising God by labor at his bench"—reunites spiritual and material values. The overall message is the integration and integrity of work within God's purposeful reign: "Teach us how to do all work for God."

Broad and deep biblical perspectives on work underscore humanity's creation and redemption in God's social image. In the Hebrew Scriptures work is a God-given expectation. Most theologians who do, address the workplace in the biblical context of creation, pointing to the injunction in Genesis to production and reproduction—Be fruitful and multiply, and fill the earth and subdue it" (Gen. 1: 28a)—as well as to the explicit command in Exodus:

> Six days you shall labor and do all your work. But the
> seventh is a sabbath to the Lord your God; you shall
> not do any work. (Ex. 20:9-10a)

Clearly in this and other texts work by itself, apart from God and time for divine praise and thanksgiving, does not make life worth living. Trying to discover the meaning of work was apparently a biblical as well as a modern concern. The Book of Ecclesiastes, written around the second century B.C.E. amid confusing civil and social conditions, claims that although toil is a gift from God, like wisdom, pleasure, and riches, it is *not* the end and value of life.

Another biblical emphasis reminds us that work must not
be turned into a means of oppression, a way of dehumanizing
others. The central biblical event of the Exodus has variously
been described as a labor dispute, a "walkout," and the re-
lease of workers from oppressive landlords. The liberation of
workers is underscored by James Weldon Johnson's version
of the Exodus in *God's Trombones*, where Pharaoh's wife
complains:

> Pharaoh—look what you've done.
> You let those Hebrew Children go,
> And who's going to serve us now?
> Who's going to make our bricks and mortar?
> Who's going to plant and plow our corn?
> Who's going to get up in the chill of the morning?
> And who's going to work in the blazing sun?
> Pharaoh, tell me that![2]

The Old Testament prophets, particularly Amos and Isaiah,
rail against those who live in luxury off the labor of the poor.
"What do you mean," Isaiah challenges, "by crushing my people, by grinding the face of the poor?" (Is. 3:15). Amos attacks
the greed of those in a deceitful, acquisitive society who
"trample on the needy...for a pair of sandals" (Amos 8:4-6).
The connection here and elsewhere between "profits and
prophets" is more than a pun: Scripture's concern for the social order mandates ethical scrupulosity in dealing with oneself and with others.

The household laws of the Torah also seek to set limits
upon the burden of work through three institutions: gleaning
rights, the Sabbath, and the Jubilee Year. Farmers were obliged to leave provisions in their fields for the needy and vulnerable:

> You shall not reap to the very edges of your field, or
> gather the gleanings of your harvest...you shall leave
> them for the poor and alien. (Lev. 19:9-10)

Vineyards, orchards, and fields were to lie untended every seventh year so that the land itself could be rejuvenated (see Ex. 21:24; 23:10-11; Dt. 23:24-25; 24:19-22), while the vision behind the Year of Jubilee (every forty-ninth year) sought renewal of society as a whole. Not only would the land lie fallow, but also slaves were to be freed, debts cancelled, and wealth redistributed (Lev. 25:23-24). Such provisions place work and economy within perspectives of both justice and renewal. Indeed recreation is part of divine creation; like God, workers also rest from their labors. The Hebrew Scriptures not only address exploitation, they emphasize respect for the land and its laborers as well.

The everyday material world is also the context for the teachings and parables of Jesus. American Roman Catholic bishops, in their critically informed and helpful 1986 Pastoral "Economic Justice for All," observe that Scripture invites all Christians to meet God "in the world of farming and fishing, of buying and selling, of weddings and feasts." Despite this clear grounding of biblical teaching in the social order, modern interpretations of New Testament texts tend to divorce the message from the original context. The contemporary theologian Dorothee Soelle says that modern preachers make the mistake of "spiritualizing" particular texts that address economic issues. Such interpretations err by making a false separation between material and spiritual values, thus seeking to limit or confine the power of biblical teaching about wealth and poverty.

The social context of first-century Palestine was marked by increasing concentrations of wealth under Herod's policies of confiscating lands, trade, and exports, and levying high taxes in order to consolidate and extend his reign as a vassal king of the Roman Empire. Biblical scholar and sociologist Gerd Thiessen. describes a widening separation between upper and lower-class values in communities of the Jesus movement. Intense political instability resulted as the fragile religious liberties of these conquered people were affected by Herodian court intrigues and the shifting fortunes of Roman rule. Thiessen names the overriding social issues of these communities, not unlike our own, as political revolution (intense political turmoil), peace (demilitarization), benevolence (the desperate need of charity for the poor), and human value (religious rights in particular).[3]

That is the context in which we should read the parable of the Laborers in the Vineyard, a teaching tale which, among other purposes, reveals work as a measure and sign of God's generosity. In this parable a landowner hires laborers early in the morning for the "usual daily wage." When the landowner sees other workers standing around in the marketplace, he also hires them—some at noon, some at three o'clock, and some as late as five o'clock. At the end of the day he pays all of his workers the same wage, but those who were hired first grumble, saying:

> "These last worked only one hour, and you have made them equal to us who have borne the burden of the day and the scorching heat." But he replied to one of them, "Friend, I am doing you no wrong; did you not agree with me for the usual daily wage? Take what belongs to you and go; I choose to give to this last the same as I give to you. Am I not allowed to do what I choose with what belongs to me? Or are you envious because I am generous?" So the last will be first, and the first will be last. (Mt. 20:12-16)

This parable is full of biblical assumptions about labor, some subtle and others more direct. Jesus' contemporaries understood a reference to "the usual daily wage" to mean the amount of money it took to support a worker and his family for a day. This was the central basis for determining wages, from biblical to pre-industrial times. In other words, for this parable a daily wage is one that sustains life. Today's far different standard relates wages instead to the market exchange value of a laborer's product or service. The notion of impoverished laborers, "working poor" who are unable to provide themselves with the basic necessities of food and shelter, was unacceptable to this parable's landowner. Thus to send a laborer away without an adequate daily wage, no matter how long that person had worked, was untenable.

This parable also underscores the vision of a society where all who are willing and able to work are welcome. It is a story about the economy, literally, the "household of God," where none are left idle and God's graciousness extends to all who seek a livelihood.

While the Hebrew Scriptures speak to making provision for those unable to work, this and other New Testament texts confirm the message that a humanizing economy provides work for those able to labor. Such work not only supports the survival not only of individual laborers and their kin, but also benefits the wider community. It is in this everyday world of vineyards and markets that those who labor will meet God and find salvation. Values about work and workers in the full promise of biblical theology are as expansive and generous as the message of redemption in Christ.

"Faith and Work"

According to a recent survey, many members of American church congregations struggle to draw direct and supportive connections between their work lives and their church membership. However, the respondents saw a much clearer connection between religion and family affairs. The researchers were left wondering whether work life seemed too "material" or "not religious enough" to integrate with faith. They relate the response from a member of a board of directors who, when challenged about the ethics of a particular business practice in his firm, replied: "Morality? What does that have to do with it? This is business, not sex."[4] To strengthen interactions between faith and work, these researchers suggest each denomination should identify not only biblical but other

traditional theological resources that inform ethical understandings of the workplace.

The Incarnation provides one such positive resource. Indeed, for much of the last two centuries this doctrine has informed theological reflection on work and laboring society as
a whole. Perhaps we have forgotten or neglected the story of
how English theologians, facing the social and economic crises occasioned by newly-industrialized British economy,
turned to the Incarnation for aid in interpreting society. In his
study *Social Teachings in the Episcopal Church*, Robert
Hood calls this a startling omission:

> For a church proud of its ecclesiastical tradition and
> theological legacy via the Church of England, it is all
> the more surprising that even the theological social
> thought and thinkers coming out of 19th century An-
> glicanism have seldom been points of reference for
> shaping and critically examining Episcopal social
> teachings.[5]

I wish to redress briefly this lapse in our denominational
memory. This allows me the privilege of introducing (or rein-
troducing) you to two of the greatest Anglican theologians:
Frederick Denison Maurice and William Temple. From the
1840s to the 1940s, these two theologians presented influential Anglican perspectives on the emerging industrial and social order. The result of their work was not a specific
program, but rather an attitude about the interrelationship of
faith and work. Their opponents advocated withdrawal (or at
least a critical distance) from public life and society, but
Maurice, Temple, and their associates emphasized public
Christian responsibility and social concern. They argued,
pointing to the Incarnation, that God did not stand aloof from
the material conditions of human; the church, like Jesus, has
good news for the poor, not merely the well-to-do. Both
Maurice and Temple turned to the doctrine of the Incarnation
with its emphasis on the power of God's ongoing creation

and the promise of Christ's transforming presence at work within humanity.

In the middle of the nineteenth century Maurice (whose name is pronounced "Morris") observed the crisis caused by the rapid extension of the Industrial Revolution throughout Victorian society. Class divisions were escalating between wealthy entrepeneurs and the laboring poor, particularly in the heavily industrialized north of England. Contrasts and conflicts grew between newly rich Victorian gentlemen and newly organized British working classes. The stench and horror, the riches and opportunities possible in this increasingly polarized society are graphically portrayed in the novels of Charles Dickens, particularly *Hard Times* and *Nicholas Nickleby*.

Maurice believed widespread social breakdown was rooted in theological breakdown. He suspected that many Victorian theologians had lost sight of Christ's transformative power in human society, and wrongly emphasized human sinfulness:

> The fall of Adam—not the union of the Father and the Son, not the creation of the world in Christ—is set...as practically the ground of [the] creed.[6]

Instead, Maurice's starting point was the Trinity, and more specifically Christology.

> My desire is to ground all theology upon the name of God the Father, the Son and the Holy Ghost, not to begin from ourselves and our sins; not to measure the straight line from the crooked one. This is the method I have learned from the Bible. There everything proceeds from God....I have maintained that Christ, by whom, and for whom all things were created, and in whom all things consist, has made reconciliation for [us].

Maurice accepted Christ as the archetype of humanity. For gentry and laborer alike, Christ was the head of humanity, the ground of Christian life in this world.

Maurice taught neighborliness rather than individualism as the appropriate social goal. This was not a naive, simplistic rejection of individuality; rather, he challenged all claims to superiority and believed that "competition...put forth as the law of the universe...is a lie." Competition should be replaced by cooperation and efforts to abolish, rather than endure, suffering and injustice. Maurice emerged as the forerunner of those who later advocated and developed Christian Socialist programs. Throughout his life Maurice and the English theologians who followed him in the struggle for social justice argued that the doctrine of the Incarnation forced Christians to take the temporal needs of the world as seriously as it took the spiritual.[7]

William Temple was perhaps the most distinguished twentieth-century churchman and ecumenicist; he served as Archbishop of York and later Archbishop of Canterbury during the Second World War. In the middle of the twentieth century Temple argued it was not only the right but the duty of Christians to interfere in social issues. His best-selling book, *Christianity and the Social Order* (1942), advocated heeding the church's voice in the realm of politics and economics. This powerful and distinctly Anglican stance is poles apart from the attitude held by many Christians today, which is exemplified by a letter I recently received from a woman who insisted that the church had no place in the social order because the Bible was "about peace between man and God, it says nothing about peace between man and man."

Temple based his affirmation of Christianity's role in the social order not only on repeated biblical injunctions to "love your neighbors," but upon his belief that the Incarnation imbued humanity with a new spiritual power touching all of human life: public and private, material and spiritual, individual and social. The work environment, and not only the home, was a good place to put faith into practice. Temple believed that through the Incarnation Christ "inaugurates a new system of influence," a natural and "final stage of evolution" emphasizing social interdependence:

> Humanity is a close-knit system of mutually influencing units. In this sense the humanity of every one of us is "impersonal."[8]

He explicated this "impersonal" role of self-interest as intimately social, urging contemporaries to order their lives so that "self-interest prompts what justice demands." We are, in other words, truest to "Christ within us" when we perceive all of daily life—at work, at home, at church, in the public sphere—as means of expressing God's will. "Christianity," Temple once realistically noted, "is the most materialist of all the world's great religions."

The Incarnation's affirmation of creation, emphasizing the sacredness of human life, also deepened Temple's catholic, sacramental perspective on work. He envisioned the sacramental power of the eucharist calling forth humanity's mutuality; he spoke of the bread and wine as our "industrial and commercial life in symbol." This theological emphasis on the dignity of daily human life, created and imbued with God's presence, shaped Temple's reflections on work, its organization and reform, and the larger values of the social order. For both Temple and Maurice, an affirmation of human striving as the site of divine activity provides the foundation for a theology of work. Maurice, Temple, and others associated with this tradition of social thought affirmed not simply the church's ability to address issues of the workplace and wider society, but even more the potential of Christ's incarnating love to transform human culture. The enormity of their vision is apparent. Just think of it: a culture in which the eucharistic bread and wine, not a Coke bottle, symbolize the mutuality of all workers.

Another way to illustrate the distinctive nature of Anglican attitudes toward faith and work is by exploring how they differ in emphasis from other approaches. Contemporary theologians Joseph Holland, a Roman Catholic, and Protestant M. Douglas Meeks both identify a tendency in modern American culture to denigrate work as a material curse on humanity.[9] From this perspective, religious meaning is found by transcending work. It is a viewpoint that rests on a sharp division between "religious" and "secular," and it occurs both in traditional Catholic thought and in sectarian theologies. Disdain for workers, clericalism, and romantic views of religious vocations are some of the consequences of denigrating labor. Holland, for example, notes that Roman Catholics used to assume mental labor was more heavenly, and manual labor more earthly, while ordination was the highest vocation. Maurice and Temple alike rejected this kind of disdain for workers, emphasizing that the Incarnation elevates all of humankind.

A second modern ideology, one which particularly (though not exclusively) attracts Protestants, tends to exalt work as a means of ordering and gaining justification. Most of us know someone who believes that working hard is a sure way to win divine approval. This perspective is part of our cultural heritage. Theologically it focuses on the individual, isolated worker's efforts to find security through productivity. But what about those who don't work, such as children, the frail elderly, or those who seek work but are unable to find it? Are they outside God's justification? Moreover, as Meeks notes, exalting work's saving power contradicts the traditional Protestant affirmation of justification by faith in God's redeeming love. Maurice and Temple rejected an emphasis on individual worth through productivity, and pointed instead to the communal and social character of labor.

There is a related and more secular perspective which, while not theologically derived, is a common attitude toward work and the social order. This ideology—found alike in writings of Hegel, Marx, and many modern economists—elevates work as the source of meaning in life. This perspective suggests that work can be redeemed through correctly ordering and managing the economy. This modern ideology tends to emphasize not the dignity of workers but their efficiency and productivity within a market economy. In this technological view, human labor becomes an objective element in production; laborers are no longer inherently valued as God's subjects. Parker Palmer, a contemporary teacher of spirituality, cites an ancient poem by the Taoist teacher Chuang Tzu that goes straight to the heart of this issue:

> Produce! Get results! Make money! Make friends!
>   Make changes!
>   Or you will die of despair.

Managers and workers who adhere to this advice, Palmer observes, become "prisoners in a world of objects."[10] Incarnational theology, instead, emphasizes our subjectivity as children of God, redeemed bearers of God's gracious love.

Holland identifies within Roman Catholic thought a fourth perspective on work. This theological emphasis calls for renewed attention to the honored place workers hold in the scheme of creation. Holland traces this "new tradition" from its early beginnings in the 1891 encyclical *Rerum novarum* (usually called "On the Condition of the Working Classes") to John Paul II's 1981 declaration in *Laborer Exercens* ("On Human Work") that "human work is a key, probably the essential key, to the whole social question" and the 1991 encyclical *Centisimus Annus*, which affirms the church's concern for social and economic thought. Holland urges Christians to envision work as part of a fully integrated, religious perspective:

> All work is profoundly religious, even if we are not conscious of that fact. Work is nothing less than human participation in the divine creativity expressed in the creativity of the universe.[11]

Renewed Roman Catholic emphasis on the significance of work is an important and positive contribution for Anglicans and other Christians. It recalls Temple's insistence on identifying work and its place in the social order as central to religious life.

This review of modern perspectives on work helps to clarify Maurice's and Temple's contributions in balancing and integrating attitudes toward faith and work. As we have observed, most theologies of work (including recent Roman Catholic thought) focus on creation and on the products and results of human labor. The danger here, particularly in modern economic systems that elevate work as the source of meaning in life, is that laborers come to be valued primarily for their service to larger economic goals. Anglican theology provides an important corrective to modern theologies of work by emphasizing that humanity's true nature is affirmed through the Incarnation; Maurice, in fact, suggested that the Incarnation had theological priority over creation. When evaluating the human situation—and work is close to the practical heart of the human life—he insisted that "Christ precedes Adam" in serving as the redeemer of his own creation. From Temple's perspective as well, the Incarnation was the mighty act through which God affirmed creation.

What Anglicans have to contribute to a theology of work is an incarnational emphasis upon the Christ within us who affirms the essential dignity of workers. In this perspective the values of creation and incarnation cohere, allowing focus on both workers and the products of their labor. There is a clear christological focus to Anglican theologians' perspectives on work. The full promise of the story of Christ's incarnation, including atonement for our sins, negates our efforts to seek redemption through work. Meeks concludes:

> Released from work as frenetic self-assertion, the justified person can enter into work as free service of God's grace.[12]

Incarnational theology, and the metaphor of "Christ the worker," model the hope of laboring for God's realm on earth. Once we claim what Maurice called "our true center in Christ," we can discover the real value of working interdependently with God and one another to carry forward the great work yet to be done.

The image of Christ "teaching us how to do all work for God" illustrates Maurice's and Temple's vision of the unity of the spiritual and material, their affirmation of human striving, and their emphasis on the coherence of work and faith. Their theology of work is evoked in a verse by one of Temple's favorite poets, Rudyard Kipling in "When Earth's Last Picture":

> And only the Master shall praise us, and only
>   The Master shall blame;
> And no one shall work for money, and no one shall
>   work for fame.
> But each for the joy of the working, and each
>   in his separate star,
> Shall draw the Thing as he sees It for the God
>   of Things as they are!

"The Workaday World"

Incarnational theology fully recognizes the mystery and promise of "the God of things as they are." Yet the actual environment and general experiences of workers in the United States are not easily described—and not only because workers' lives are diverse and variable, although they are indeed. Nor is it because the economic structures that provide the context for labor in America have shifted significantly in the last decade, perhaps more than during any other decade in this fast-moving century. Nor is it because simply initiating conversations about expectations of work touches for most people strong, personal feelings—including unexamined and at times painful reflections on their own social class and background.

Talking about work is also difficult because there are culturally normative assumptions governing our working lives that mask reality. The trouble with many of the old definitions is they don't work any more—and maybe they never did. As Gilbert and Sullivan playfully opined in *Trial by Jury*, "Things are seldom what they seem,/ Skimmed milk masquerades for cream." In an interview with Sam Keen on his recent book, *The Mythic Journey*, the Protestant theologian describes negative myths and false assumptions that are guiding our lives. Such myths, he says, "disidentify truth," binding us in ways we don't even recognize; we insist, "That's just the way it is." The dominant modern myths, Keen claims, are economic. He points to moments of embarrassed silence and evasive humor when the question of money comes up, and asks, "Why is it so hard to talk about money?"[13] We have a good deal invested in controlling our feelings and assumptions about work, money, and vocation. As you review the following statistics and stories, I invite you to reflect carefully on your history as a working person and to keep track of your assumptions, challenges, and questions.

Sketching the current working environment involves three tasks: naming some of the dominant myths about the workaday world, underscoring recent changes in the U.S. economy (the structural foundation for work), and describing major shifts in the character of employment in North America. To accomplish even this brief review of work I will call on a wide variety of experts, keeping in mind what Richard Hooker said back in the sixteenth century about the need to draw on diverse sources of knowledge:

> [Wisdom's] ways are of sundry kinds, so her manner of teaching is not merely one and the same. Some things she opens by the sacred books of Scripture; some things by the glorious works of nature: with some things she inspires them from above by spiritual influence, in some things she leads and trains them only by worldly experience and practice (II.1.4).

Anglican bishops at the 1988 Lambeth Conference similarly defined reason's teaching authority to include the poet, the painter, the psychologist, the economist, the philosopher, and the scientist. I wish to utilize a wide range of observers—economists, political scientists, sociologists, and journalists to discern realistic perspectives on "things as they are" in today's world of work.

One of this culture's dominant myths about work is its creed of individual success. Anyone can make it in America, it is said, through hard work, guts, and gumption; effort and ambition are all that is needed. In this view of success, not only is each person divorced from the larger social context with its powerful economic structures and trends; but this principle—traditionally stated as "Every man for himself"—can breed competitiveness and lack of trust. That is why managers spend an inordinate amount of time checking up on employees. Yet another implication of the myth of personal success is the assumption that self-made people are solitary and do not have to cooperate with others. Incarnational patterns of interdependence and mutuality have little chance in such an environment.

The modern-day Horatio Alger rags-to-riches stories with their myth of individualism and personal success ignore the fact many of our hardest workers have the lowest incomes. Hard times do not hit everybody the same. Kevin Phillips, a widely respected Republican political analyst, describes the Reagan years as "the best of times, the worst of times" in pointing to the two most visible economic groups of the 1980s: billionaires and the homeless. Demographers are identifying a large and growing group of Americans they call the "structural poor," those with few chances to escape from poverty.[14]

Another, related myth that blunts the realities of working life is the assumption of American "classlessness." The misleading insistence that most of us are in the same boat is analyzed by Benjamin DeMott in *The Imperial Middle: Why*

Americans Can't Think Straight About Class. Politicians, including George Bush, have campaigned on the notion, "Class is for European democracies....Class isn't for the United States." Yet sociologists and economic analysts are observing widening social differentiation. Over the last twelve years the poorest fifth of the American population grew poorer, while the richest fifth became richer; currently the top ten percent of families owns seventy-one percent of America's wealth, while ninety percent of the rest of us own the remainder. A noted economist believes that rich and poor Americans inhabit different economies, and predicts that the top "fortunate fifth" is departing from its interest in and engagement with the rest of the nation.[15] This report of increasing class polarization is similar to first-century Palestine, another context in which incarnational principles of social interdependence and neighborliness were proclaimed.

Another myth at the heart of society, Sam Keen observes, is its insistence that the American economy depends on increasing consumption patterns. "That's just the way it is," you might be thinking, yet we have in fact changed from a nineteenth-century culture of production to a contemporary culture of consumption. Justification for this kind of economy has imminent scarcity as its starting point: many contemporary market economists also view human nature as not only acquisitive but "naturally insatiable." According to Parker Palmer, the social result of economies built around the assumption of scarcity is a decline in neighborliness and community:

> Competition (a way of allocating scarcity), rather than cooperation (a way of sharing abundance), is widely regarded as the only way to conduct our affairs, to make things happen. How else can you explain the fact that our country so fearfully clings to its habit of overconsuming the world's resources, as if letting other people have a fair share would mean national suicide? At every level of our lives the assumption of

scarcity, not abundance, threatens to deform our attitudes and our actions.[16]

Compare these assumptions to those of the divine, economic household; they are radically different. Amos and other socially-minded prophets implied that where righteousness and justice are found, there is enough to go around. Scarcity is usually caused by injustice. The illusion of absolute scarcity not only prevents social interaction, but grounds modern market economies in greed.

One "supermyth" supports these and other assumptions about the contemporary social environment for work. That is the assertion of our technological capacity to control ecology, the economy, health, and even human destiny. Palmer describes it as the myth that tells us "all things are plastic, malleable, capable of being molded into any shape we require or desire."[17] Sources of this destructive assertion are egotism and arrogance. I am reminded of a *New Yorker* cartoon picturing one five-star general remarking to another: "It really shook me, I can tell you. I dreamed the meek inherited the earth!"

Instead of these misguided and dangerous assumptions, we can find surer grounds for incarnational perspectives on work by reviewing current North American occupational trends. We have indeed come a long way: from a society of food gatherers, to one based on care of animals and crops; from agricultural to early industrial and product-driven economies; and, most recently, from an industrial to an information society in which knowledge-intensive occupations are replacing all others. Only one in four North Americans are employed in industrial pursuits, while the service sector—finance, insurance, real estate, business, government, and, increasingly, health—provides seven out of ten American jobs. In a major and influential reassessment of the national economy, Robert B. Reich describes three occupational groupings: first, what he calls "industrial routine production services," which are now disbursed throughout the world to take advantage of the least expensive sources of labor; second, direct "in-person service positions," which are health care, janitorial, restaurant, child care, and hotels, for which there is growth primarily in lower-skilled occupations; and third, the fastest growing occupational segment of "symbolic-analyst services."[18] The latter are highly educated positions calling for specialized knowledge and skills to fit precise needs, such as trouble shooters, strategic brokers, and those who can identify new solutions. If we wish to understand and support social policies encouraging today's workers, it helps to be realistic and specific about shifts in job distribution.

It is also helpful to be aware of two large-scale structural changes in the economy that have themselves altered occupational patterns. U.S. manufacturing, first of all, has become increasingly marginalized, with capital instead moving into financial speculation and services; today it represents only a fifth of total national income. With productive forces shifting into Third World countries, the U.S. economy is moving away from traditional production, with primary emphasis in this country on selling luxury products. We are no longer first in producing goods from cars to ships, or from steel to machine tools; over all, economists speak of the "deindustrialization" of the U.S.[19]

The second major shift is the globalization of the economy, including so-called multinational corporations. While politicians and others tend to blame U.S. economic problems on the declining competitiveness of American companies, it is probably more accurate to observe that national corporations are ceasing to exist in any way that can be meaningfully distinguished from the rest of the global economy. This is the major and persuasive premise of Robert Reich's analysis in *The Work of Nations*. In 1989, for instance, the president of NCR Corporation brushed off worries about U.S. competitiveness, describing NCR as a "globally competitive company that happens to be headquartered in the United States."

I grew up in the environs of Detroit. We were a "Ford Family" through and through; my father served "old Mr. Ford" and his grandson from the early 1930s through the 1970s. Today the successful efforts of Ford and other automotive giants no longer center on high-volume production in this country, but on the provision of specialized knowledge and services to others. As a passionate automotive "nationalist" for most of my life, I find the following dissection of a new car's genealogy surprising and fascinating:

> When an American buys a Pontiac Le Mans from General Motors, for ex., he or she engages unwittingly in an international transaction. Of the $20,000 paid to GM, about $6,000 goes to South Korea for routine labor and assembly operations, $3,500 to Japan for advanced components (engines, transaxles, and electronics), $1,500 to West Germany for styling and design engineering, $800 to Taiwan, Singapore, and Japan for small components, $500 to Britain for advertising and marketing services, and about $100 to Ireland and Barbados for data processing. The rest—less than $8,000—goes to strategists in Detroit, lawyers and bankers in New York, lobbyists in Washington, insurance and health-care workers all over the country, and General Motors shareholders—most of whom live in the U.S., but an increasing number of whom are foreign nationals.[20]

We may believe we are "thinking globally, but spending locally," yet the reverse may be more accurate. If we seek through our economic arrangements to live into a relationship of radical interdependence modeled in the Incarnation, we may have to rethink our starting point.

Another, more familiar way to describe the shifting environment for U.S. workers is to review those job populations traditionally called "blue-collar" and "white-collar." In general, blue-collar employees are a diminishing breed, outnumbered three to one by white-collar workers. Two-thirds of the blue-collar positions created since 1970 pay less than $13,500 a year, and the so-called fringe benefits of health insurance and pensions are increasingly rare. With the poverty line in 1990 set at $12,700 for a family of four, it is not surprising that statistics indicate increasing numbers of "working poor"—persons with jobs that fail to provide a living wage. Many of these workers are the parents of those poor children we identified in our discussion of childhood poverty. There is also a resurgence of blue-collar juvenile workers. In 1990 nearly six thousand firms were cited for illegally employing forty thousand minors, and this epidemic of child labor abuse, fueled by the global demand for cheap labor, is increasing.

Interviews with a wide range of workers recounted by Studs Terkel and Barbara Garson relate similarities in the emotional landscape of blue-collar workers. Working-class jobs commonly do not allow room for creativity, and often are subject to heavy-handed, demeaning supervision. One women describes her job this way:

> Well, this one woman Viola fainted at nine-thirty and she was really sick. But her house was out of the city limits. So they said, "We can't have someone take the time off to take her home."...It's this kind of thing that makes you feel bitter....Why should you put out, when you're nothing to them as soon as you stop skinning fish? You're not even as good as a machine, because they wouldn't leave a broken machine just sitting on a bench in the locker room.[21]

There are also repeated testimonies about the loneliness, isolation, and self-estrangement involved in routinized work, as from this spot welder at a Ford plant:

> You pretty much stay to yourself. You get involved with yourself. You dream, you think of things you've done....Repetition is such that if you were to think

114

about the job itself, you'd slowly go out of your mind.[22]

Many jobs, in the name of efficiency and control, are actually designed to keep people apart.

Of course, you may be thinking, conditions are quite different among white-collar workers. There are differences as well as surprising similarities. The persistent economic tendency is reduction of jobs and replacement by machinery. White-collar jobs are disappearing or being downgraded—the management term is "de-skilled"—to more repetitive operations often involving technical electronic equipment. Garson describes this trend among telephone workers, salaried brokers working for "financial supermarkets," and "automated" social workers. White-collar positions that were once characterized by lack of close supervision are increasingly subject to intensive monitoring. An airlines reservationist reports:

> They monitored you and listened to your conversations. If you were a minute late for work it went into your file. I had a horrible attendance record—ten letters [over four years] in my file for lateness, a total of ten minutes.[23]

The occupational middle class, sociologists observe, is disappearing, becoming increasingly "bipolar" with statistically few good jobs at the upper-level management end and the rest relatively de-skilled.

Even those with jobs that are not physically or routinely alienating, such as successful middle-class professionals, are reporting emotional dissatisfaction. Theologian James E. Dittes writes in *When Work Goes Sour* that much professional work ultimately fails to satisfy because managers and others often take professional skills for granted. Additionally he points to a prevailing cycle of stress and workaholism:

> You just can't leave work alone....You work all day, all evening, and all weekend and still feel anxious, if

you take time off for church or a movie, about the
work that is overdue and undone....Like alcohol,
work numbs even while it offers the illusion of vital-
ity.[24]

Working as a compulsive life-style is another consequence of
elevating work as the source of life's meaning.

From these and other reports we might conclude that most
workers hate their employment, and that alienation is struc-
tured into the very character of work, and for some occupations this is so. Yet investment, creativity, and the desire to
make a contribution keep reappearing in workers' stories.
Garson indicates that despite resentment, routine, and mo-
notony, "the most dramatic thing I found was quite the opposite of noncooperation. *People passionately want to
work*."[25] Terkel records a gritty, hard-driving interview with
a steel worker who muses for a rare moment on how he
would like to see his back-breaking work commemorated:

> I would like to see a building, say the Empire State,
> on one side of it a foot-wide strip from top to bottom
> with the name of every bricklayer, the name of every
> electrician, with all the names....Everybody should
> have something to point to.[26]

Not only is work an expectation, even if some manage to
escape from it; most people, blue and white-collar workers
alike, want to do a fair day's work. In large measure—whatever our daily occupation—most of us invest in work with a
mixture of pride, tough realism, humor, and a sense of want-
ing to make a larger contribution. A Chicago garbage collec-
tor wryly observes that people are

> just too stupid to realize the necessity of [this] job....I
> don't look down on my job in any way. I couldn't say
> I despise myself for doing it. I feel better at it than I
> did at the office. I'm more free. And, yeah—it's mean-
> ingful to society. (Laughs.)[27]

Despite alienation, diversity, stress, and changing character of the working world, the bottom line is: "People passionately want to work."

This basic desire makes layoffs and unemployment, increasingly widespread among many occupations, all the more painful. Whether blue- or white-collar, full- or part-time, at home or in the public arena, the desire to contribute through intentional labor is a norm, so much so that non-workers (graduate students, for example) are usually regarded with suspicion. Yet full employment for those seeking work is not a goal of the U.S. economy; indeed, it is considered "healthy" to have between six and eight percent unemployment, although less than three percent is due to temporary imbalances between supply and demand. Today's high unemployment rates would not have been tolerated twenty years ago; between 1939 and 1976 there were only two years when unemployment rose above six percent. Nor is there a dependable assistance program through unemployment insurance: only thirty-seven percent of unemployed persons receive benefits, while those of more than one million people have run out (they are called "exhaustees" by the Bureau of Labor Statistics).[28]

Exhaustion, depression, and despair are appropriate states of many persons searching for work. I have observed devastating, broad swings of unemployment in the Detroit area and I also watched my former husband bear the stigma of being without work for two long periods early in our marriage. Again and again I shuddered as colleagues and peers would literally stop listening to him when—in response to the frequently asked question, "What do you do?"—he would reply that he was looking for work. Rather than to address structural economic issues related to job loss, many Americans tend to dismiss unemployment as an individual problem created by those deviants who "could find work, it they *really* wanted to." In conversations about work it is important to hear and attend to voices of the unemployed. From the incarnational perspective of God's identification with the human condition, everyone—regardless of their working history—counts in ethical descriptions of the workaday world.

"Holy Living"

The modern world of work with its vast diversity is a complex, changing, and, for many American workers, troublesome environment. Neither simplistic pleas to connect work with faith, nor idealistic praise from pulpits for laity who engage in "Monday's ministries" do justice to the challenge of making a living. Given today's shifting and abrupt economic realities, can we offer courage and support for workers? How can we engage the larger cultural issues of the workplace while speaking with the distinct voice of our own theological tradition? Practically speaking, what can congregations do to strengthen bonds of work and faith? Is it helpful, for example, to address new perspectives on work in church as well as in the workplace? Can we offer pastoral care for those blue- and white-collar workers who experience alienation in the workplace? How do we bring our behavior and expectations into line with the social teachings of our faith?

Again history is helpful. Anglicans and other Protestants carry as part of their religious inheritance the larger Renaissance and Reformation emphasis on valuing each person's active occupation. Thomas a Kempis' late fifteenth- and sixteenth-century "best-seller," *Of the Imitation of Christ*, advised "working at something useful for all in common." Whether a "priest or hangman," Luther quipped, all Christians are called to service amid neighbors and community. Increasingly in the Protestant Reformation the term "vocation," or intentional calling, was used to refer to laity as well as clergy. Jeremy Taylor, a seventeenth-century Anglican divine, was known and admired for meditations addressing the practical duties of daily life. In *The Rule and Exercises of Holy Living* (1650), Taylor spoke of being ordained to life. "All employment," he noted, "is sacred if well lived."

Let us review for a moment how thinking incarnationally about workers informs "holy living." While Anglicans are not alone in emphasizing the dignity of laborers, our sacramental life provides regular opportunity to reflect on the sacred and shared meaning of human life. It may be useful for you, as it is for me, to recall Temple's reference to the eucharistic bread and wine as collective representations of "industrial and commercial life," symbols of the work we are given to do. Other incarnational principles and insights for working persons underscore criticism of competitive individualism, advocacy of interdependence among workers (Temple's "higher stage of evolution"), and redefining self-interest to emphasize social identity, creativity, and generosity. This is a rich, challenging legacy for a theology of work and for grounding social policy.

You might want to review your own assumptions about work, workers, and contemporary environments for labor to see what other concerns or questions come to mind. It might be helpful to ask, for example, does *all* work have positive value or meaning? Here again incarnational insights are helpful. Occupations that contradict God's intent for human nature, that are dehumanizing of others, or destructive of community well-being, should be scrutinized closely. Yet the issue of work's value, or lack thereof, is not always solved easily. Luther, for example, did not question the value of a hangman's vocation, but today many would disagree. When we affirm the integration of work and faith, congregations can become places where members enter more deeply into discussion about ethical dimensions of the workplace.

In addition to thinking incarnationally about work in general and your own work in particular, I have four other applications in mind that contribute to the dignity and well-being of workers. At the top of my list is the resolve to stop casting blame on individuals who are unable to find work; instead I would prefer that we address unemployment as a profound theological and societal problem, as well as a personal struggle. In God's intended realm, none of those seeking work are left idle. I imagine God grieves over the unused talent and creativity of those left jobless. Dorothee Soelle observes, "To deny someone necessary and fulfilling work is to deny that person's being created in the image of God." Given the high rates of unemployment in this country, it is time to listen critically and respond publicly to the wide variety of suggested remedies and structural changes for creating new jobs.

Second, the incarnational criterion of participating with dignity in God's ongoing creation, encourages me to pay closer attention to the social dimensions of the work process itself. Practically speaking, this suggests not taking workers for granted, addressing alienation both through constructive support and repeated affirmation of skills, and supporting workers' rights to influence the organization of their labor. Self-estrangement in work and isolation in labor are antithetical to human wholeness, which is an ideal lying at the heart of the Incarnation.

Viewing work through the lens of incarnational theology can also lead to asking very tough questions: for example, Is trusting workers a possibility? There are new and partial managerial responses—variously called "economic democracy" and "workplace democracy"—that affirm the active decision-making by all who labor. These range from women's descriptions of "interactive leadership" to initiation of small-group management teams that set and work on their own goals. In such situations, however, the basic structure of work usually does not change.

A more radical alternative is provided by a Boston-area chocolate company—with 150 people on the payroll and a worth of three million—that relies on trust as a powerful management tool:

> All work in an atmosphere of complete trust—no time clock—no credit checks—and no secrets. . . .The Harvard Business School says, "You've built a new culture."[29]

The founder of this company reports his banker advised him (after his firm exceeded a million dollars in profits), "This trust nonsense will have to stop." Suppose all workers were truly stewards of their labor? What the Bible requires of stewards is they be "found trustworthy"(1 Cor. 4:2). A sane moral theology of work—focusing on the dignity of human beings—involves not only access to decent, honorable, productive work, but also a say in how that work is organized.

A third concern I have for reenvisioning work in light of incarnational perspectives involves regaining the regenerative cycle of labor and leisure. The God of creation both worked and rested, yet many of us seem to think we are better off working the whole week long. This tendency toward workaholism, it appears, is a distinct U.S. temptation; on average we have stingier paid vacation policies than other advanced countries, including Japan. Thomas Merton believed that overwork was one of the most pervasive forms of contemporary violence:

> The rush and pressure of modern life are a form, perhaps the most common form, of its innate violence. To allow oneself to be carried away by a multitude of conflicting concerns, to surrender to too many demands, to commit oneself to too many projects, to want to help everyone in everything is to succumb to violence. More than that, it is cooperation in violence.[30]

Howard Thurman had similar thoughts. His meditation "Lest Your Activity Consume You" concludes, "The wise man...lives his life seriously each day but he does not take it seriously."[31] Parker Palmer warns against succumbing to a "vacation approach to life," plunging into a vacation and then back again into activity; he advocates a major perspectival change, with regular integration of contemplation and action. I am reminded of the Benedictine Rule's wise, rhythmic movement of work, study, and prayer. Labor without provision for leisure is dehumanizing. Without resting places, no road is worthy of travel.

My thoughts have so far turned to steps I could initiate in the working environments of my own life. Yet the relationship of radical interdependence modeled in the Incarnation and so admired by Maurice and Temple implies a deeper change in normative social assumptions about work. What if the framework for work itself were not primarily an individual's job, but the larger human community instead? What if work reminded us of the shared meaning of all social goods? This would necessitate a significant shift from possessive individualism to redefining work as socially self-interested service to the larger community. Temple would concur with dramatist and statesman Vaclav Havel, who addressed these words to the U.S. Congress:

> Without a global revolution in the sphere of human consciousness, nothing will change for the better.... We are still incapable of understanding that the only genuine backbone of our actions, if they are to be moral, is responsibility—responsibility to something higher than my family, my country, my company, my success.[32]

Havel, like Temple, advocates thoroughgoing reconsideration of the social order.

For Christians, making a living is seldom a simple goal. The Incarnation provides a theological reminder that life essentially is a sacred gift. Included in this gift is the chance to work. "Holy living" involves entering into the graceful freedom of this gift. Anglican perspectives on work move us toward "Christ the Worker," reminding us once again that God in Christ is the continuing ground of our justification. An incarnational theology of work underscores Christ's transforming presence:

> Maurice may help us to understand that the responsibility of contemporary theology is to make clear the

hidden power, the inner meaning, the real substance, of *all* happiness is the event of Christ... [the] *eternal* word of God's unconditioned love.[33]

This happiness includes other gifts as well. Toward the end of the nineteenth-century Industrial Revolution, novelist George du Maurier wrote in *Trilby*:

A little work, a little play
To keep us going—and so, good-day!

A little warmth, a little light
Of love's bestowing—and so, good-night!

It is now time to turn from work to even more intimate reflections.

Endnotes

1. The words of this Ghanaian song were translated by an African missionary, Thomas Stevenson Colvin; see *The Hymnal 1982*, #611.

2. James Weldon Johnson, *God's Trombones* (New York: Penguin Books, 1983), p. 50.

3. Margaret M. Mitchell, "Social Teaching and Social History: Learning from the Early Church," *Christian Century* (August 2-9, 1989), 724-25; see Gerd Thiessen, *The Sociology of Early Palestinian Christianity*, trans. John Bowden (Philadelphia: Fortress Press, 1978).

4. Stephen Hart and David Krueger, "Faith and Work: Challenges for Congregations," *Christian Century* (July 15-22, 1992), 683-86.

5. Robert Hood, *Social Teachings in the Episcopal Church* (Wilton, CT: Morehouse Publishing, 1990), p. xviii.

6. Most of the quotations cited below from Maurice are conveniently available in William J. Wolf, ed. *The Spirit of Anglicanism* (Wilton, CT: Morehouse-Barlow, 1979), p. 75. For an introduction to Maurice, see pp. 49-98.

7. A review of the policies and theologies of those who, like Maurice, argued social action should not be separated from sacramental life is found in John Richard Orens, "Politics and the Kingdom: The Legacy of the Anglican Left," *Anglican Theological Review*, LXIII, No. 1 (1981), 21-41.

8. Most quotations from Temple are cited in a biographical and theological essay by Owen C. Thomas, "William Temple," in Wolf, *Spirit of Anglicanism*, pp. 101-134.

9. On the denigration of work see Meeks, *God the Economist: The Doctrine of God and Political Economy* (Minneapolis: Fortress Press, 1989), pp. 134-39, and Joe Holland, *Creative Communion: Toward a Spirituality of Work* (New York: Paulist Press, 1989), pp. 7-17. I owe the naming and description of these perspectives on work particularly to Meeks, pp. 139-51.

10. See Parker J. Palmer, *The Active Life: A Spirituality of Work, Creativity, and Caring* (San Francisco: Harper & Row, 1990), pp. 37-38.

11. Holland, *Creative Communion*, p. 36; pp. 18-24.

12. Meeks, *God the Economist*, p. 149.

13. Sam Keen, *Fire in the Belly: On Being a Man* (New York: Bantam Books, 1991), p. 238; Keen includes an excellent inventory of questions about work and money that apply to women as well as men.

14. Kevin Phillips, *Politics of Rich and Poor: Wealth and the American Electorate in the Reagan Aftermath* (New York: Random House, 1990), p. 3; see also Jerry Kloby, "The Growing Divide: Class Polarization in the 1980s," *Monthly Review*, Vol. 39, No. 4 (September 1987), 2-7. The structural poor, growing in numbers, are disproportionately urban, African American, and Hispanic, although overall there are more whites in this category. See Allan Ornstein, "Urban Demographics for the 1980s: Educational Implications," *Education and Urban Society*, Vol. 16, No. 4 (August 1984), 486-87.

15. Benjamin DeMott, "America's Dirty Little Secret: Class," *The Boston Sunday Globe* (November 25, 1990), A25-26; Kolby, "The Growing Divide," p. 4; and Robert B. Reich, "Succession of the Successful," *The New York Times Magazine* (January 20, 1991), 16, 42-45.

16. Palmer, *The Active Life*, pp. 125-27.

17. *Ibid.*, p. 69.

18. Robert B. Reich, *The Work of Nations: Preparing Ourselves for 21st-Century Capitalism* (New York: Alfred A. Knopf, 1991), pp. 82-86, 196-97.

19. Bertrand Bellon and Jorge Niosi, *The Decline of the American Economy* (Montreal: Black Rose Books, 1988), esp. pp. 9-11 and 66-69; this restructuring process removes the industrial base from the cities, leaving a different pattern of urban dwellers. See Ornstein, "Urban Demographics," pp. 481-88.

20. Reich, *Work of Nations*, p. 113.

21. Barbara Garson, *All the Livelong Day: The Meaning and Demeaning of Routine Work* (New York: Penguin Books, 1975), p. 39. See also Andrew Levison, *The Working-Class Majority* (New York: Penguin Books, 1974), pp. 58-68.

22. Terkel, *Working*, p. 222; see also Garson, *All the Livelong Day*, p. 24.

23. Terkel, *Working*, p. 83; see also Barbara Garson, *The Electronic Sweatshop: How Computers Are Transforming the Office of the Future into the Factory of the Past* (New York: Penguin Books, 1988), pp. 71-154.

24. James E. Dittes, *When Work Goes Sour* (Philadelphia: The Westminster Press, 1987), pp. 39-42.

25. Garson, *All the Livelong Day*, p. xi- xiii.

26. Terkel, *Working*, p. 2.

27. *Ibid.*, pp. 150-53.

28. Long-term unemployment is consistently underestimated. On economic bases of unemployment see Richard A. Easterlin, "The New Age Structure of Poverty in America: Permanent or Transient?" *Population and Development Review*, Vol. 13, No. 2 (June 1987), 195-208; also on the pervasive character of unemployment see Kenneth Root, "Job Losses: Whose Fault, What Remedies?" *Research in Politics and Society*, Vol. 3 (1988), 65-74.

29. This and the following quotation are excerpted from unpublished papers by Benneville N. Strohecker, the firm's founder.

30. Thomas Merton, *Conjectures of a Guilty Bystander* (Garden City, NY: Image Books, 1968), p. 68.

31. Howard Thurman, *The Inward Journey: Meditations on the Spiritual Quest* (Richmond, IN: Friends United Press, 1980), pp. 71-72.

32. Quoted by David Nyhan in "At Long Last, Some Lips Worth Reading," *The Boston Sunday Globe* (February 26, 1990), A23.

33. Contemporary theologian Schubert Ogden, quoted in Wolf, *Spirit of Anglicanism*, p. 49.

5

Power in Flesh

Incarnational Perspectives on Intimacy

One of my mother's favorite sayings was, "Thou art neither cold nor hot; thou art lukewarm, and I spew thee forth." It took me years to realize this saying actually came from the Bible, from the Book of Revelation, and it is directed against the complacent, self-satisfied faith of the Roman inhabitants of Laodicea (Rev. 3:16). To my youthful ears, however, they were my mother's words; if she had not invented them, I was quite sure Shakespeare had.

Mother was an actress: she was very dramatic, outgoing, and prone to resonant pronouncements. She loved "character," as she called it. Vibrancy, passion, energy, and eccentricity were all admired; boredom and complacency were lurking enemies. The idea of being "lukewarm" was nauseating to her, much as it was to the author of Revelation. I recall as a young child coming home from school distraught and complaining to her about a demanding teacher. I've forgotten the teacher, but I still remember Mother's disarming reply: "At least," she said rebuffing my juvenile plea for pity, "*this* teacher caught your interest!" Then I heard those words once more, "Thou art neither cold nor hot, thou art lukewarm, and I spew thee forth." The relational patterns of my childhood home were similarly strong, dramatic, and impassioned; the leading characters, as I now recall them, were all larger than life.

Church too played a central part in this drama. The vast, compelling parish of my youth was Christ Church Cranbrook, Bloomfield Hills, Michigan. As children we learned to say this name rapidly, without pausing, like one big surname: Christ-Church-Cranbrook-Bloomfield-Hills-Michigan. In my memory this parish was never "lukewarm," and it seldom occurred to me that church could be boring (at least for long). Each Sunday I would rush to greet Diantha, the guiding spirit of the church school (her official title, I later learned, was Director of Religious Education), whose loving laughter was infectious. What's more, she challenged us to try new things: when I was an adolescent, she encouraged me "to teach" my first class, kindergarten. Of course there was also a preacher, named DeWitt, whose stories we sometimes heard, but I was quite sure Diantha was in charge.

Religious leaders in my childhood were family friends. These companions were fully engaged with members of the parish, much like the God whose huge pictorial story greeted us every Sunday. There, behind the altar of this parish church, was a mural depicting the partially clothed results, in living color, of God's energetic intervention in human affairs: crucifixion, resurrection, salvation, and damnation were all part of the unfolding drama. During church services I studied the details of this vast panorama, sometimes looking for women and children (there were few) and other times counting angels, yet always caught up by the particularity of these enfleshed, life-and-death images. During Sunday school, guided by a challenging curriculum called the Seabury Series, I learned about the "mighty acts of God"—stories of a deity who was distinctly *not* "lukewarm." Therefore I have never understood those theologians who suggest that God is above the fray, a kind of "non-controversial gentleman" who prefers to stay out of the passion, confusion, and disorder of human affairs. God was not represented this way in my family, in Sunday school, or in our altar mural. Vibrant pictures of life and death, the full range of human emotion and experience, were part of being Christian, part of being what from my Anglophile parents I later learned to call "Anglican."

These seeds, deeply sowed in childhood, bloomed later in my life. As an adult I have learned, and am still learning, to come to terms with intimacy: the close, sensuous, enfleshed, and sometimes conflicted nature of human relationships. In this area of growth I am not alone. Intimacy is a powerful topic for many of us; it is seldom a "lukewarm" subject. For instance, when in conversation we refer to our most "intimate needs," we may well have several things in mind: the need to feel loved, understood, accepted, or supported, as well as the need to express ourselves sexually.

Definitions are helpful. When we are talking about personal matters—and theology is always personal as well as corporate—no one wants to be misunderstood. In proper English, "intimacy" does not refer to an abstract, private space. The dictionary says intimacy means "pressing into"—touching and defining—the heart of a matter, whether it is a profound "intimate" understanding, the unique characteristics of an "intimate" relationship between two people, or the corporate "intimacy" that church members express as they engage one another. Intimacy touches and informs the identity of individuals, groups, and parishes. Intimacy, then, is not neutral. It is a kind of knowledge about the self, and it presumes knowledge of others. Intimate knowledge is at the heart of human relationships, reflecting our expectations not only of one another, but ultimately of God.

Intimacy is the larger context for our most personal relationships, with sexuality as one of its components. Based on the total witness of Holy Scripture, sexual expression lies within the scope of our created gifts for intimacy. Like other divine gifts, sexuality can be used for joyous as well as destructive ends. Once again, definitions are helpful. In common parlance the term "sexual" is frequently misconstrued as referring only to specific genital activities. Instead, I use the word "sexual" to designate a whole range of erotic, embodied feelings, energies, and activities. More careful observers and experts also give wider definitions to the word "sexuality," including the ways we live as male and female in a culture with particular gender expectations, feelings, and attitudes about our bodies. "Sexuality," thus broadly defined, is one of the many aspects of intimacy, and it involves and invites intimate knowledge of others.

In this chapter I have chosen to focus on sexuality within the framework of intimacy, rather than on sexuality as narrowly construed. This is intentional. For me intimacy is an ideal larger framework in which to view sexuality, particularly for those of Jewish and Christian heritage. This frame of reference is truer to the ideals and principles of the Incarnation. A God who, in Christ, partakes of the fullness of human life is a God who bears the full range of love's power, including the capacity to instill and invite devotion, passion, affection, and friendship. A God who through the Incarnation reinforces the understanding that our bodies are good, is a God who intends sexuality as one of numerous sources of pleasure, celebration, and nurture.

There is yet one more reason why intimacy, including sexual intimacy, unlocks incarnational principles. Theologically and practically, pressing into the heart of things invites images of death as well as life. One of the most intimate experiences of my adult life was the death of my former husband

and lifetime friend, Bruce. I remain tender about his death from AIDS and about the struggle he experienced throughout this illness to stay faithfully connected to family expectations. Although he, too, was raised as a church-going Anglican, his upbringing could not have been more different from mine; he was encouraged to see his body and its functions as separate, as "disincarnate," from his true nature. This legacy, however, did not stop Bruce—much later on in the process of his mature living and dying with AIDS—from eventually rediscovering a profound truth: he was in fact a whole, incarnate person. Throughout his final illness, Bruce realized he did not merely *have* a body but *was* a body; his body was not to be ignored or downgraded in sickness or in health. Incarnational theology reinforced for him the embodied fullness of humanity.

For my own part in the midst of Bruce's life-threatening illness—which included insightful "good" days as well as painfully hard "bad" ones—I was reintroduced to the healing power and promise of the Incarnation. I should not have been surprised by the closeness of death and intimacy. They are, after all, familiar companions in biblical story and religious verse. Since that time I have rediscovered George Herbert, a seventeenth-century English poet and herald of emerging Anglican spirituality. Herbert's verse is affirmingly rich with intimate imagery of God:

> My God, what is a heart?
> That thou shouldst it so eye, and woo,
> Pouring upon it all thy art,
> As if thou hadst nothing else to do.

Herbert's unique power as a poet includes the capacity to hold together things mistakenly believed to be separable; he does so with a sure, direct simplicity that encompasses the theological complexity of life and death:

> Come, my Way, my Truth, my Life;
> Such a Way, as gives us breath:

Such a Truth, as ends all strife:
Such a Life, as killeth death ("The Call").

Similarly, the contemporary Guatemalan poet Julia Esquivel declares, "how marvelous it is to live/threatened with Resurrection!" She speaks of the paradoxically empowering sense of "liv[ing] while dying...already know[ing] oneself resurrected."[1] An American lyricist bluntly notes, "The soul afraid of dying will never learn to live." The intimacy of God's love, as I reaffirmed with Bruce, invites us to confront the fear of death. Along the way, I trust, Bruce and I also learned that Christian life in Anglican perspective is neither outward or inward, nor physical or spiritual, but inescapably both. Whether in dying or living incarnational theology is part of a movement toward human wholeness.

In particular and in general, intimacy and Anglican theology have much to do with one another. At the heart of human relations is intimacy, marked by sensuousness and passionate, embodied sexuality, the desire to reach profound understanding, and the rich, mysterious complexities of human relationships. At the heart of Anglican belief, worship, and theology is the Incarnation: a deeply mysterious yet emphatically promising story of a God whose life among us provides a basis and a demand for ongoing responsibility as Christians.

When inquiries about intimacy and incarnational insights are placed side by side, the event of Jesus, "power in flesh," takes on new life and promise. In the first chapter I described the ways an incarnational lens could color depictions of God, humanity, and the continuing relationship between the two. In this chapter I wish, first of all, to sharpen the focus of these portrayals with particular reference to intimacy, and review for a moment the incarnational "good news" of God's impassioned nature, humanity's redemption through Christ, and the criteria of responsive mutuality in creation. Next, I intend to identify historical and other patterns that too often block us from gaining intimate knowledge, keep us from asking questions about everyday experiences of intimacy, and over time prevent us from incorporating in full the incarnational legacies of God's love. Finally, I will suggest some transforming perspectives that can faithfully ground personal and corporate expressions of intimacy. Much as the lens of the Incarnation proves constructive in looking at habitual attitudes toward childhood, aging, and work, this incarnational prism can illumine and transform assumptions about our most intimate experiences.

The impassioned nature of a "God of Love" is inescapable. Herbert's poem "Evensong" underscores the strength and accessibility of this persistent love:

My God, thou art all love.
Not one poor minute scapes thy breast,
But brings a favor from above;
And in this love, more than in bed, I rest.

It is this divine, welcoming love that Herbert celebrates in "The Call":

Come, my Joy, my Love, my Heart:
Such a Joy, as none can move:
Such a Love, as none can part:
Such a Heart, as joys in love.

Herbert's poetic insight accords with the central biblical legacy of a passionate God who longs for relationship with humanity. Modern Asian theologian Kosuke Koyama also describes a passionate God of creation who through the Incarnation "becomes vulnerable because of God's intense love for humanity." Koyama adds that this biblical God "neither engages in sexual acts nor has a spouse," and yet is the gracious creator of human sexuality. Verna Dozier underscores the theme and image of God "the lover":

At the heart of the biblical understanding of God [is] a lonely God, a vulnerable God, a God who loves....God chose a relationship that involved love—lover-beloved.[2]

From the jealous creator God of Exodus (Ex. 20:5) to the shepherd searching for the one lost sheep (Lk. 15:4), the large biblical canvas presents an impassioned God whose heart "joys in love." It is in this intimate likeness we are created.

When we turn from the story of the first Adam of Genesis to the second Adam of the gospels, intimate metaphors and images persist. We need not spend our time in speculation about Jesus' "sexual life"; in fact, to frame the question in such a way sounds not only profane but ridiculous. A person's "sexual life" is grounded and expressed in a much fuller developmental context than any short description or label can capture. This is yet one more reason why I prefer to think about sexuality as an aspect of human intimacy. It is enough to underscore the fact that the story of incarnation embodies God in human flesh: "And the Word became flesh and lived among us."

Verna Dozier helpfully reminds us, "God did not become incarnate as a book, but as a person." So it is not surprising that the dominant metaphor chosen by the biblical Jesus—the model and the context in which Jesus in the Gospel of John invites and commands responsive sharing from those he calls disciples—is "friendship," a category drawn from intimate human relationships:

> You are my friends if you do what I command you. I do not call you servants any longer because the servant does not know what the master is doing; but I have called you friends. (Jn. 15:14-15a)

In this compelling text, love is a dynamic relationship, a two-way exchange of energy. Followers of the risen Christ are not colleagues, or neighbors, or work associates; they are called friends.

Friendship is not for those who like to dwell on nostalgia and sentimentalism; there is nothing sweet about the loss of a best friend, a really close friend, whether through misunderstanding or through death. An incarnational God who in Christ shares life with us involves us in interdependence, responsibility, reciprocity and risk, giving and taking, pain and struggle. We know too that Jesus' expansive love was frequently viewed as scandalous, causing Pharisees and others to murmur against him: "This fellow welcomes sinners and eats with them" (Lk. 15:2).

The affirming spirit and legacy of God's continuing presence in our lives is shaped through the ultimate sacrifice of friendship: the son of God offering his life to redeem all God's children. Through the Atonement all aspects of created humanity, including sexuality, are redeemed for responsible life in the New Creation. This saving act underscores God's intent in calling forth humanity to serve in the totality of creation's gifts. Leonardo Boff speaks of humanity as redeemed into the "archetype of Christ" and thereafter gifted with the capacity for "infinite relationship with God." Redemption offers the graceful possibility of responding to divine love with our own. God does not require excessive scrupulosity; as F. D. Maurice insisted, new life comes through living in the light of Christ's redemptive action, not by dwelling on Adam's fall. Anglican theologians from Richard Hooker to Desmond Tutu reiterate God's longing for humanity to live not in sinfulness, but in "redemptiveness."

The unfolding story of the Incarnation envisions a renewed intention for human and divine mutuality, mutuality grounded in intimate knowledge of others. Koyama envisions sexuality as one intimate mode among others for expressing mutuality:

> The sacred meaning of sexuality is not located in sexuality itself, but rather in human mutuality. Sexuality is a mode in which human mutuality is expressed.[3]

There are other purposes for human sexuality, including procreation. Yet envisioning sexuality as a created, incarnate gift from God—reaffirmed in redemption—necessitates the criterion of mutuality.

Right use of intimacy in sexual relationships invites interdependence. The embodied God who lives and loves among us cares about our intimate relationships, about the way we use this and other created gifts. Much as William Temple, guided by incarnational principles, recast self-interest as social interest, so too intimacy has an undeniably communal base. From childhood to old age, intimacy is relational, and involves the consent and the knowledge of others. When individual fulfillment is divorced from care of others, there is increased potential for neglect and abuse. Intimacy, like any other God-given freedom of expression, is grounded in awareness of others, of a wider family or community. Whatever other criteria Christians affirm for expression of intimacy, including sexual intimacy, its location in mutually affirming relationships should clearly be at the top of the list.

Seen through the lens of incarnational theology, intimacy is both singular and social, seeking and inviting reciprocity. Maurice once spoke of the inherent ability of Anglican theology to reunite diverse elements that, however distinct, were never meant to be separated. In the same way Leonardo Boff points to a "courage for incarnation" that lies at the heart of all catholic Christianity, the courage to mix "heterogeneous elements" and to experience "the divine...made present through human mediation."[4] As we have seen in the last chapter, incarnational theology resists fragmentation, the separation of social from spiritual concerns. Anglican theology also embraces a reunited, coherent understanding of spirituality and intimacy, including sexual intimacy. The overall promise of incarnation affirms we are neither in this life, nor in the next, nor in our most intimate relations, to be separated from the love of God. A God of such impassioned, persistent love would have it no other way.

"A Difficult History"

These general reflections may not sound controversial. Yet Christians across the centuries have fought over their application, positing this or that expression of intimate human relationship as naturally meritorious, with others as inherently evil. Today many people still find it extremely difficult to participate in conversations of any sort about sexuality. Despite the prevailing affirmation of Scripture that sexuality is an essential part of our created human nature, more negative assumptions persist in implying that human sexuality is dangerous if not sinful for religious people. As a result many of us are denied opportunities to gain critical theological perspectives about intimacy from conversations in our homes and parishes.

As we have seen, theology at its most constructive touches and presses upon the realities of daily living. Our biblical and Reformation ancestors believed that theological knowledge was a source of practical understanding and strength, helping them address local questions and close wide gaps of understanding in their lives.

Unlike them, we live in a culture where theology is not widely discussed. Yet church members today have their own worrisome local questions, and several of them are about intimacy: questions, for example, about fidelity in marriage, about AIDS, about teenage sexuality, about domestic violence and sexual abuse, and about diverse lifestyles. If we wish to address these and other questions, as well as learn from incarnational and other theological resources, we may have to overcome difficult institutional and cultural prohibitions about discussing intimate concerns.

A lot of people say they have a bad history with mathematics, while any number of others complain they have a difficult history with history. "I just can't remember all those dates," they say. To which I, as a teacher of church history, reply that we do not have to remember the things we can look up. The Christian church has a difficult history with sexual intimacy. Look it up! James Nelson, a social ethicist whose scholarly works provide sustained reflection on human embodiment, believes that "churches have not been able to deal creatively and forthrightly with sexuality in virtually any form." Nelson suggests most denominations approach sexuality as the medical system does illness: both are "more oriented to disease than to health."[5] This leaves church members little opportunity to develop abilities to distinguish between healthy and unhealthy expressions of sexual intimacy. In some churches, as in some family circles, discussion about an entire range of intimate needs is off-limits.

It is possible to read the history of Western Christianity, a popular U.S. magazine recently suggested, as a dramatic conflict between so-called sexual and spiritual "sides" of human nature. We are not so away far from the late-Victorian piety of my maternal grandmother who looked down on human bodies and was equally confident heaven was completely spiritualized. Grandmother, who was a Methodist, once took great offense at an Episcopal funeral sermon on the resurrection of the body. So if we wish to confront this difficult history as late twentieth-century Christians, we can begin by questioning and ultimately discarding inaccurate aspects of traditional Christian history. In addition to misguided historical assumptions, there are other maxims and perspectives that prohibit wider understanding of human intimacy. As Black poet and theologian Audre Lorde reminds us, "The master's tools will never dismantle the master's house." I propose identifying unhelpful tools and other obstacles, modern and traditional, blocking us from increasing our theological awareness of human intimacy.

Scholars are not sanguine about gaining accurate historical impressions on topics like sexuality. Most admit to the strongly selective memories of various cultures. Much as when we reflect on our own family's history, there are events we tend to remember, while others are excluded. This creates a kind of imaginary zone that others can fill in with stories and scripts of their own devising. Modern scholars recognize that traditional histories concentrated exclusively on powerful and successful persons at the expense of the more marginal; history can read, Jane Austen once noted, as if it were invented "without any women at all." Christina Larner, an historian of popular religious beliefs during the English Reformation, describes the result of excluding inconvenient historical information:

> The effect of this is that we cannot see past systems of thought as connected wholes. We single out those aspects which we have inherited for applause and those we have discarded, for special explanation....In such partial identification we invent the past.[6]

If historical data, one source for information on valued traditions, does not envision people and their cultures as "connected wholes," then it is no wonder we have inherited fragmented ideas about the personal practices and beliefs of our ancestors.

Additionally, historical evidence about the lives of ordinary people—those heralded neither as saints nor as notorious sinners—is either nonexistent or consistently weak. Yet one of the most frequent claims of moralists is that we have strayed today from "traditional sexual ethics." When I read such claims, I can imagine historical people receiving our simplistic reports of "their" standards with bemused laughter, if not outright confusion. Stereotypes, historical and contemporary, are by nature and intent misleading.

Distorted historical assumptions about marriage practices in Western Christian cultures are a case in point. What we do know about marriage rites in the "good old Christian days" is not good news; there are few liberating guidelines. Typically, biblical, medieval, and Reformation stories about marriage are—except for the miracle at Cana—steeped in hatred of women. Many biblical stories illustrate the two bases of power which, according to anthropologist Claude Levi-

Strauss, have determined the cultural dominance of men: the exchange of words and the exchange of women. Thus Catholic and Protestant marriage ceremonies have largely evolved from practices based on the exchange of property, women, and other social goods. Not until the thirteenth century was there much acceptance of matrimony as a sacrament. Wealthy laity, in particular, took advantage of the church's assistance to guarantee marriage contracts. Common law marriage, or unsanctioned cohabitation, was the norm and not the exception until property was broadly disbursed. To this day, exchange of property is the primary reason for the legal regulation of marriage contracts and their dissolution.

Instead of invoking historic, traditional values about marriage, I suggest we turn to central biblical guidelines about just, loving relationships. Biblical scholar Walter Wink writes:

> There is no biblical sex ethic. The Bible knows only a love ethic, which is constantly being brought to bear on whatever sexual mores are dominant in any given country, or culture, or period.[7]

Many people today look upon marriage as a partnership intended to express and give love form. It is a process, similar to the Incarnation, that invites the realization of love and not just its inspiration. The continuing story of incarnation does not end with the wonder of God's nativity, any more than a marriage is defined by the beauty of one's wedding. Giving love form is a process that takes time. Biblical narratives about God's love, including those shaped by the Incarnation, present realistic models more than distorted histories and sentimental beliefs.

Another of the "master's tools" to discard or at least to place in proper context is the historical and theological equation of sin with sexuality. Why, if much of the biblical record is neither anti-nature nor anti-body, does post-biblical Christianity regard human sexuality as the fault of humanity? One short answer, historian Peter Brown explains, is that Christians today are heirs of a "heavy legacy" of early Christian and medieval anthropology with its central distrust of sexual pleasure. Augustine of Hippo—a key player in the process of antiquity's conclusions about sexuality—believed that descendants of Adam were marked not only by the consequences of Adam's sin, but by the sin of sexual desire, concupiscence itself. Another modern historian, Elaine Pagels, characterizes Augustine's increasingly influential interpretation of "original sin" as theologically disastrous.

How did this notion take root in the popular and learned theological discourses of antiquity? Brown says it stems from an early popular notion that being possessed by the Holy Spirit canceled (or should cancel) sexuality activity. Clergy and others who desired spiritual transformation were increasingly drawn to limit or renounce sexuality and advocate celibacy. This is not the full background to the complex origins of the doctrine of original sin and its equation with human sexuality. There were early Christian theologians (Irenaeus, for one) who argued that Christ's incarnation and cross set humanity free. Yet Augustine's "heavy legacy" has often prevailed; indeed it was revived as part of the Christian renewal moment we now call the Reformation, and debate continues today as well.

Some might object that by challenging Augustinian legacies of original sin, I am implying that humanity is not prone to sinfulness. Not so; the theological tool I recommend discarding is the assumption that human sexuality is the root metaphor for sin. This is not a biblical assumption, but the product of theologians who feared and distrusted women, as St. Augustine did when he wrote that a woman was a "misbegotten male." Umberto Eco's novel about monastic life and learning in the Middle Ages, *The Name of the Rose*, portrays women as whores, witches, or both. This pathological view became entrenched when institutional Christianity assimilated historical events as divine law, and turned cultural norms into so-called natural law. At such times the imaginary, the real, and the symbolic have been powerfully and intentionally blurred to give the appearance that religious authorities were doing something about sin. It is long past time for modern Christians to discard remnants of other cultures' anthropologies.

Part of our ongoing historical and theological housecleaning should involve reclaiming root biblical metaphors for sin. In Hebrew Scriptures the frequent metaphor for sin is injustice, the refusal to love God and one's neighbor. In the New Testament, as John Snow recalls in *Mortal Fear*, the "most powerful metaphor for sin is captivity to the fear of death. Those ruled by the fear of death will do anything to stay alive."[8] From the perspective of incarnational theology, sin is the refusal of relationship with God and those God loves, the refusal to accept the fullness of grace "we have all received" (Jn. 1:14-16). Verna Dozier also defines sin relationally:

> Sin is a misuse of human freedom that separates us from God, from other people, even from ourselves. In fact our very concern about other people's sins is a manifestation of sin. Sin is separation. The wholeness of creation is broken.[9]

In these and other definitions, sin is not equated with sexuality per se; rather, sin is identified as intentional disobedience to God's created, incarnate, and continuing expectations for humanity. This brief review of Western culture's difficult history reminds me of a related set of power tools I would like to excise. Subordination separates, yet built into the structures of Western social thought, literature, philosophy, and psychology is a preference for oppositional, "either/or" assessments that reinforce it. Contemporary French feminists Helene Cixous and Catherine Clement identify a series of destructive dualisms that they describe as a "double braid" around the necks of all who seek to be fully embodied lives: culture over nature, day over night, head over heart, form over matter, thinking over feeling, male over female, master over slave, parent over child, white over black. Cixous and Clement also recall Freud's reinforcement of patterns of domination within our most intimate relationships through his belief that inequality, not equality, "triggers desire" in sexual relationships.[10] These are the obstacles that lie in the path of mutually supportive intimacy.

There are also contemporary theological and literary habits and attitudes that further prohibit our understanding of human intimacy. Perhaps the most personal work involves giving up egocentricity about our own identity as sexually intimate persons, because the way we define ourselves can become a barrier to welcoming others. Here I wish to draw an analogy to ethnocentrism: the practice of considering the beliefs, values, and customs of other people and cultures only from our own viewpoint or that of our culture. This narrowness is depicted and mocked in Robert Louis Stevenson's "Foreign Children," from *A Child's Garden of Verses*:

> Little Indian, Sioux, or Crow
> Little Frosty Eskimo
> Little Turk or Japanee
> O! don't you wish that you were me?

The parallel I have in mind between ethnocentrism and sexual intimacy leads me to coin the word "sexualcentrism." I intend this word to express the habit of disparaging the sexual relations of others because they are not our own.

In an article on intimacy, ethicist Robert Cooper warns against having such a high view of marriage that it "usurps" other forms of intimacy.[11] The belief that marriage is by nature and divine law a superior state for everyone is heterosexist. When this belief is founded on personal experience, I would call it "sexualcentric" as well. We can hear other hints of "sexualcentrism" in comments like these:

> Aren't all single persons lonely? Where do they spend the holidays?
> Shouldn't marriage be a criteria for ordination? My

wife has made my ministry possible and the priesthood is such a lonely vocation.
Don't all gay men and lesbians have unhappy childhoods? I am grateful my mother loved me!
My father shouldn't live with her. She's younger and
will exhaust him physically.
I don't know what's wrong with you young people.
Why would you want to live together before marriage? We didn't.
It's too bad AIDS is spreading to normal persons, like
us, who don't deserve to get it.

This last comment illustrates how deadly stereotyping can
be. Stereotyping an "other" leads to robbing that person, or
group of persons, of any reality; they are made into the image
of an "enemy," a legitimate target for aversion, exclusion,
degradation, and violence. Racism, homophobia, sexism, anti-
semitism, and genocide are all born of personal and cultural
stereotypes. In *As We Are Now*, her shocking novel about
ageism, May Sarton observes, "How wrong we are to permit
ourselves any stereotype where human beings are con-
cerned."[12]
Projection is another, somewhat different form of sending
inappropriate signals about sexuality and other intimate aspects of human life. When a young child, for example, swings
her head down, looks up between her knees at the world,
and says: "Mommy, look! Everything is upside down!" she is
projecting her view on the world, teasing her parent with a
silly conclusion. Yet in reference to sexuality, projection is
seldom benign. Historical theologian Margaret Miles in *Car-
nal Knowing: Female Nakedness and Religious Meaning in
the Christian West* describes how for centuries men have
looked at a woman, or at the picture of a naked woman, and
declared, "She's out to seduce me!" In earlier centuries
women who "looked like" witches—with or without their
clothes on—were burned. Today, theologian Carter Heyward
claims lesbians and gay men have become "scapegoats of

[our] larger society's inability to deal honestly with sexuality." It is in the nature of prejudice, Catholic ethicist Dan Maguire cautions, to condemn what we do not understand. When we project fear and confusion on others, we also deny their basic right to self-representation.

There is one more pathology that has been given a new twist. Preoccupation with individual fulfillment is not new, although "self-esteem" may well be a modern, made-up word. What is new to my historian's eyes is an exaggerated approach to self-fulfillment that individualizes widespread social problems and turns the focus away from tough, inevitable social complexities and tensions of daily living toward intensive self-scrutiny. Not all of life's problems can be translated into personal issues to be solved by personal will alone. A single-minded focus on personal esteem has led some proponents of personal "recovery" to conclude that we need to shield and protect ourselves from ethical claims placed on us through caring for others. Popular psychologist John Bradshaw, for example, implies that relationships are not interactions we enjoy, but experiences we survive:

> The only way we can find out if we really matter to someone is to stop taking care of them. Then and only then can we see if we matter for no reason at all, no better reason than that we are.[13]

Imagine trying this advice out with a frail, elderly parent, a neglected and psychologically distressed child, or an AIDS buddy. This dangerously heightened focus on the self encourages individual adults to make unreal distinctions between care for others and care for themselves. The disturbing emphasis here is similar to the choice Carol Gilligan describes as so unhealthy and destructive in the moral development of adolescent girls. We must be attentive to the danger of moral detachment from others in our efforts to focus on any individual's restoration to health. I have no brief against the modern Twelve-Step movement, from which I have personally benefited, yet when any approach to healing becomes preoccupied with the isolated individual, the wider context is endangered. It may be helpful to remind ourselves that the word "individual" literally means an "undivided whole." I suspect the so-called sexual immorality of our day has very little to do with particular sexual lifestyles, but a great deal to do with our failure to challenge assertive notions of individualism. Seen through the lens of incarnational theology, intimacy is both singular and social, inviting responsibility and reciprocity.

The ultimate consequences of all modern brands of intense focus on individualistic self-fulfillment—whether in our most intimate relationships or in the workplace—are moral, social, economic, and spiritual detachment. Within this worldview, the incarnational goals of mutuality and interdependence are either personally dangerous or distracting. If self-esteem is our culture's primary relational issue, pastoral theologian John Snow warns, then disinterested autonomy may be the only way to survive in this highly competitive, aggressive, and violent culture. Do we really think that, as whole persons, we can bypass the demanding expectation of "loving our neighbors as ourselves"? Cross-cultural studies confirm the social significance of intimacy:

> Physical nurturance of babies and young children, especially the body pleasure resulting from intimate, non-exploitive touching, is crucial to the development of peaceful and socially cooperative persons. The absence of close infant nurturance...is predictably correlated with high levels of adult violence and control needs, both individually and socially.[14]

It is imperative to reclaim the incarnational promise of growth in God's love as both singular and social.

Biblical scholar Walter Brueggemann speaks of Christians as a "what if?" people, a people called and inspired to live in the power of God's impassioned promises *now*. What if, in the many choices we are called to make, including those about our most intimate relations, we were guided by incarnational insights? What if, from the first of life through its ending, we allowed the courageous doctrine of the Incarnation to shape our understanding of relationships? What if our reflections and inquiries about human nature underscored the dignity and potential goodness of humanity, and we were actually to close the gap between creation and redemption? What if the Incarnation and *not* the Fall shaped our intimate relationships, our expectations of one another, and our mission as a church in the world? What if our lives were less fragmented between work and play, being and doing, intimacy and spirituality? In sum, what would be our identity if we lived and died as followers of an impassioned, courageously incarnational God?

We can continue as we have begun, exposing both traditional and modern obstacles that interfere with claiming strength and courage through intimate relationships. There is no need to stay locked into difficult histories and cultural assumptions. More, however, is required than discarding tools and assumptions that are no longer useful, vital though that is. What new and renewed theological and ethical perspectives come to mind? I propose turning toward transformative perspectives that are biblical in their radicality and Anglican in their incarnational persuasion.

"The Personal Presence of Christ is Everywhere"

This acclamation, "The Personal Presence of Christ is Everywhere," heads Richard Hooker's chapter on the sacraments. The incarnational themes we have reviewed and the obstacles we have identified have all in one way or another touched upon the accessibility (or denial) of the indwelling Christ in our lives. Embracing Christ's presence, as we have seen, is not an individualistic, simplistic, or sentimental intention. Courageous incarnation is an *interdependent* activity requiring, Hooker maintained, "mutual participation" between

Christ, the church, and humanity in "this present world." Intimacy, from the courageous perspective of the Incarnation, involves restoring, claiming, and engaging human life in its fullness. This basic Christian profession is represented sacramentally. Although Christ's presence permeates creation, George Herbert asks in this poem to be further instructed in sacramentality:

> Teach me, My God and King,
>   In all things thee to see
> And what I do in anything
>   To do it as to thee.

In a similar vein Hooker affirms the intimate, interdependent nature of God's indwelling presence:

> God hath his influence into the very essence of all things....All things are therefore partakers of God, they are his offspring, his influence is in them. (V. 56.5)

I am reminded of an offertory sentence from the 1928 Book of Common Prayer, "All things come of thee, O Lord, and of thine own have we given thee" (1 Chron. 29:14).

Yet how do we admit and welcome this sacramental expectation in daily living? Neither easy solutions nor a problem-solving approach will begin to reveal the sacramentality of all life or to remedy the difficult history of human intimacy we have reviewed. Respected clinical psychologist and psychotherapist John Welwood advocates a more profound approach:

> The most powerful agent of growth and transformation is something much more basic than any technique: a change of heart. This kind of inner shift can only happen when our questions or difficulties really touch us and arouse our willingness to approach things in a new way. Our problems may not disap-

pear, but they become workable because we see them in a new context.[15]

Our biblical and Reformation ancestors knew about "a change of heart," and attested to the continuing power of conversion—an inward turning toward God. Early English reformers used the Greek word *metanoia* to describe an ongoing process of conversion, a repeated turning to Christ that would lead to courage for the amendment of life, for new life in Christ. *Metanoia*, the desire to turn the heart toward God, is a central intention and action of the eucharist.

In his reflections on intimacy Henri Nouwen describes conversion as "the discovery of the possibility of love."[16] The Dali Lama, the exiled Tibetan religious leader, recently described humanity's central power and gift this way: "I believe the dominant force of human nature is human affection." "Could the truth be so simple?" a member of his audience challenged. Changes of heart can be catching, socially transforming, resulting in new life. Such intimate conversions can bring forth humanity's incarnate goodness and strength, revealing more of who we really are with one another. Most of us can recall with gratitude those specific moments when we have experienced such changes of heart.

From an incarnational perspective the more we discover and choose to draw upon our embodied, created gifts, the closer we come to the truth about humanity. The catechism of the Book of Common Prayer, which begins with a description of human nature created in the image of God, stresses the freedom to make choices. The gift of making choices is key: a blessing and a curse. We can use this freedom in our most intimate and wider social relationships to reveal God's indwelling power, or to deny it. I wish to suggest four "incarnational guidelines" to assist us in making faithful choices.

First of all, I suggest we expand capacities for attentive looking and listening. When Simone Weil, a French philosopher and mystic, recommended a way of looking that is "first of all attentive," by attentive she did not mean staring or gazing patronizingly at one another. Attentive looking recognizes tension, ambiguity, difference, wonder, and mystery. Thankfully the Judean shepherds did not try to explain away or philosophize about the wonder of the star that held their gaze. Closer attentiveness allows us to esteem even those experiences, many in the intimacy of our own homes, that we often overlook or take for granted. Such attentiveness enhances appreciation of what anthropologist Clifford Geertz calls the "thickness" of human lives and human cultures.

Paradoxically, conscientious listening is most difficult among those we believe we know best: spouses, children, close friends, and other significant partners. In her best-selling book on communication between women and men, *You Just Don't Understand: Women and Men in Conversation*, Deborah Tannen describes different linguistic patterns (she calls them "genderlects") that interfere with accurate and direct communication. We have not been conditioned to listen to men and women in the same way, and research reveals this troubling habit starts early; we interpret an infant's cry differently depending on whether we think it is a girl or boy. At the other end of life, Dr. Elisabeth Kubler-Ross—well known for her work in identifying stages of grief among those dealing with death—urges careful listening to people, not to their "stages." Attentive listening and observation reveals experience as it really is, free of prevailing assumptions about "the way things are." Intimate knowledge of others' realities can overcome denial and foster open-mindedness. It allows us to recognize and appreciate the wide-ranging particularities of God's incarnation.

Second, openness to the complexity, diversity, and mystery of human life involves calling on many sources of knowledge. Throughout this book I have turned to sociologists, economists, psychologists, physicians, gerontologists, and anthropologists as well as to theologians, poets, and biblical scholars. If we wish to know God's creation intimately, all sources of knowledge that illuminate the context of human lives are valuable. In this world of pluralistic and globally interdependent cultures, mutual understanding is advanced when the social sciences, as Robert Schreiter advises, "play the principal role of dialogue partner" with theology. In *Theological Freedom and Responsibility* Bishop Stephen Bayne insisted on learning from all sources of knowledge. This tradition of apologetics was encouraged by one of Bayne's earliest English predecessors: Reformation prelate John Jewel characterized his colleagues' broad search for truth as, "We lean unto knowledge." The social sciences are essential; they prevent us from "disincarnating" theology.

New disciplines of human knowledge are increasingly valuable, while recent scholars are also redefining and expanding the boundaries of knowledge itself. Epistemology, the science of knowledge, has benefited from insights into a broad range of ways we human beings learn from and with one another. It has been suggested that men and women often learn in different ways and perceive reality through different sets of lenses. This is the central thesis in an influential study, *Women's Ways of Knowing*, which describes multiple ways of constructing reality (or epistemologies). The authors of this volume suggest we can benefit not only from scientific and rational ways of viewing reality preferred by many men, but also from "connected knowing"; here the learner (typically a woman) subjectively participates in the construction of knowledge. Intuition has long aided discovery. If women and men wish to see one another more honestly, and see life in its wholeness, it helps to expand our ways of learning and building on one another's insights. God works now, as in the days of our ancestors, to become better known through the diverse particularity of human lives.

The wider the circle of inquiries about human life, the less likely we are to draw stereotypes about human intimacy. A third transforming perspective for courageous incarnationalists is that which develops out of a heightened appreciation of difference. Embracing incarnational theology implies not

only putting up with differences, but also valuing and cele-
brating them. Simply tolerating difference, Audre Lorde reminds us, is "the grossest kind of reform." If we are stuck at
the level of passive acceptance of others, we may overlook
the powerful and creative function difference plays in our
lives. Enhanced opportunity for genuine intimacy and wonder at God's expansive vision is fostered through acknowledging and affirming particularities of race and ethnicity,
sex, age, and social and cultural context. As we have heard
from both Boff and Maurice, appreciation of difference accords with Roman Catholic and Anglican ideals of incorporating "heterogeneous elements." Differences in a catholic
sacramental framework do not, as in dualistic systems, have
to be organized in opposition to one another. Nor should diversity be denied by resorting to transparent, superficial
cover-ups; such polite illusions actually keep us apart from
one another.

I have a twin brother; obviously we are not identical twins,
although you would be surprised how often we were asked.
Our father, acting with his sense of a lawyer's impartiality,
did all he could to make sure we were treated the same. My
brother and I were, and are, differently created; our
strengths, weaknesses, and gifts invited their own recognition, encouragement, and discipline rather than constant
comparison. "Separate but equal" does not work in theory or
in practice. Douglas Meeks, who writes such informing perspectives on work and the economy, suggests, "Equality in
the household of God means radically different persons embrace and yet remain radically different."[17] So it was with my
twin brother.

Today sex role stereotypes, as well as false assumptions
about "fairness," are breaking down. Many of us are coming
to realize, in our personal lives as in the larger society, the extent to which sexism endangers the lives of women and reinforces false expectations of men. To distort humanity is to
tamper with natural differences enfleshed in and through the

Incarnation. If we look for actual differences between women and men (not assumed differences or caricatures), we would no doubt develop a new appreciation for complexity, a heightened sense of God's creation, and a good deal of humility. Some "traditional" distinctions might remain, but there would be a number of new variations for an enriched and not impoverished humanity. Incarnational theology underscores the difference that difference makes.

A sense of flexibility is implicit in transformative perspectives on human intimacy. Flexibility is essential for theologians who wish to appreciate the full measure of human intimacy. Leonardo Boff describes flexibility (the Greek word is *kantabasis*) as a basic category in biblical theology:

> God was infinitely flexible toward humanity, accepting its reality with its undeniable limitations and onerous ambiguities....The resulting Church clothed itself in a courageous flexibility toward the Greeks, Romans, and barbarians, accepting their languages, customs, rituals, and religious expressions. It did not demand any more than faith in Jesus Christ.[18]

Anglican theology has a long record of doctrinal flexibility; the Church of England was the one Reformation body that consciously avoided becoming a confessional tradition. Its characteristic caution is evident in the 1981 Church of England Doctrine Commission recommendation: "Doctrine should be authoritatively defined as little and seldom as possible." To speak incarnationally, faith is communicated anew in the context of a living fellowship. If flexibility ceased to be a basic component of the theological reflections of churches who intend to embrace a wide catholic definition of membership, such churches would become more akin to evangelical sects.

"Relativism" is an accusation frequently made against those who hold pluralistic theological perspectives. This opposite error to ethnocentrism suggests the acceptance of all beliefs as equally true; it is not the same as flexibility. Anglicans in particular have historically and theologically lived with both Catholic and Protestant inheritances; they have a long history of making faithful (not blase) choices, and of reserving the right to learn anew and even to change their minds.

Like other Reformation traditions, Anglicans face the tension of living with the distinct contradiction between maintaining the church's authority and personalizing salvation. This inherent tension and the legacy of doctrinal flexibility can prove frustrating to those who wish their church to settle controversies "once and for all"—particularly those that have to do with the most intimate activities of others. However, this is distinctly not the Anglican way. Appreciation of doctrinal flexibility, joined with an awareness of the profound complexity of human life, ought to make us cautious about drafting either/or statements. Church historian John Booty advises Anglicans and other Christians not only to "accept creative tension" but also to "anticipate gain" from conflict and respectful dialogue.[19]

These transforming perspectives—attentive looking and listening, a wide range of sources and scholarship to illumine human lives, a heightened appreciation of difference, and a basic sense of flexibility—will bring about a deeper comprehension of personal and social realities. Renewed theological appreciation of our most intimate relationships—whether we are husband and wife, cohabiting or other significant partners, parent and child, close friends, spiritual companions—is long overdue. William Law, an eighteenth-century Anglican divine, observed, "Every place is holy, every part of life is God's...a devout life is lived in the wholeness of life."

These transforming perspectives may assist our reflections, but as my piano teacher would say of all great art, "There is no substitute for practice." Fortunately we are given sacramental means to inspire our hearts and stir our wills to action. The sacraments invite the reunion of physical (outward) experience and spiritual (inward) grace. In the eucharist, as in the Incarnation, a new intimacy and a new intention for humanity is envisioned. It is not surprising that the young, reformed English church—in its zeal to communicate with people in a language they could understand—favored the images of intimacy and embodiment. The body of Christ, the body of the church, and the human body are all linked in the eucharist. With reference to the sacraments of both baptism and eucharist, Richard Hooker described the church as "the very mother of our new birth in whose bowels we are all bred, at whose breast we receive nourishment" (V.50.1).

Furthermore, this mutuality is reiterated through the use of metaphors of connection and growth, whether the Johannine recollection of the vine and its branches, a father's love for his offspring, or a mother's life-giving nurture. Flesh and blood are indigenous to human beings; this is the site of sacramental activity. As Hooker reminded his contemporaries, the intent of the eucharist was to "change lives," not bread. Much as the story of the Incarnation changed the lives of biblical people, so too in the celebration of the eucharist human lives continue to be moved.

The intimate sacramentality of the eucharistic banquet—deep in range and wonder, rich in love, and costly in price—is for me invitingly pictured throughout the text of George Herbert's poem, "Love Bade Me Welcome":

> Love bade me welcome; yet my soul drew back,
>   Guilty of dust and sin.
> But quick-ey'd Love, observing me grow slack
>   From my first entrance in,
> Drew nearer to me, sweetly questioning,
>   If I lack'd anything.
>
> A guest, I answer'd, worthy to be here:
>   Love said, You shall be he.
> I the unkind, ungrateful? Ah my dear,
>   I cannot look on thee.
> Love took my hand, and smiling did reply,

Who made the eyes but I?

Truth Lord, but I have marr'd them: let my shame
  Go where it doth deserve.
And know you not, says Love, who bore the blame?
  My dear, then I will serve.
You must sit down, says Love, and taste my meat:
  So I did sit and eat.

Much as intimacy is the ideal context for viewing human sexuality, so too intimacy—knowledge of self, others, and God—may be an ideal concept for worship.

Neither human intimacy nor incarnational theological are easily described. The story and its interpretation are not over; there may be welcome surprises just ahead. I recently read an extended profile of Roman Catholic Archbishop Rembert Weakland, who shaped early drafts of the Bishops' Pastoral Letter on the Economy. Weakland suggests that new perspectives on human sexuality may well provide the next "Galileo" revolution in our own day, leading churches to review and revise in a positive way their teaching on subjects—for instance, women in the priesthood, and the affirmation of homosexuality—once thought contradictory to Christian belief. Certainly we have yet to understand and incorporate fully the dimensions, possibilities, and challenges inherent in being human.

In the meantime, modern Christians live amid what Stephen Bayne described as "the world's always new, always agonizing search for truth and justice." An committee headed by Bishop Bayne wrote in 1967:

That the Church be truly one with humanity and at humanity's side, and that it be seen fully to respect [human] freedom, are the two indispensable characteristics of any responsible engagement on the theological and social frontiers. Those characteristics grow out of the Church's nature. In turn, they must control the Church's response.[20]

The voice of the church, like that of individual Christians, is authentically expressed when it respects and honors this mandate.

Herbert describes the doctrine of the Incarnation as a "rare cabinet full of treasure." Yet incarnational theology must not be buried like a treasure in the ground, producing no profit (see in Mt. 25:18), for other Christians can learn from Anglicanism's theological emphasis while adding their own dimensions and applications. Distinct religious values provide points of entry into wider public discourse; they are part of what we have to contribute to the debate on the public good, to remaking patterns of our shared life. Incarnational perspectives on childhood, for example, caution us against assuming power over those who are dependent on us, and challenge the adequacy of our culture's concern for welcoming children. Theological perspectives on aging underscore the intrinsic value of human life and invite us to accept loss and growth alike throughout our lives. As with aging, experiences and assumptions about making a living raise questions about daily patterns of work and play. The complex wonder and courage embodied in the Incarnation is apparent when we focus on human intimacy. God did not choose to dwell in a "nobody." Incarnational theology invites the best we have to offer, including our fully embodied, sensuous selves.

Along the way we have also been reminded that human identity incorporates individual particularities and social realities alike. Although we have looked at various components of the life cycle, these chapters have underscored the broad interdependence of human life. New life in the image of the Incarnation is intergenerational. We are learning together—not only passing on old stories, but finding new interpretations of ancient truths. Growth is movement toward, not away from, each other. In the sixteenth century Richard Hooker asserted that nothing created could say, "I need thee not." Similarly, a young African student at the seminary where I teach describes his philosophy as an African Christian: "I am because we are; we are: therefore I am." In the process of self and social discovery, focused through the lens of the Incarnation, we have become reacquainted with a remarkably generous, impassioned God. This is a God in Christ whose immanent indwelling presence and identification with humanity challenges, informs, and inspires us. This too is a God of courageous incarnation, whose transcendant wonder we are born to welcome throughout our length of days.

Endnotes

1. Julia Esquivel, *Threatened With Resurrection* (Elgin, IL: The Brethren Press, 1982), p. 63.

2. Verna J. Dozier, *The Dream of God*, (Cambridge, MA: Cowley, 1991), p. 89.

3. This discussion of God's impassioned nature and of mutuality as the "sacred" meaning of sexuality are drawn from printed meditations by Kosuke Koyama: "May God Continue to Bless Us," *Christian Century* (April 26, 1989), 442, and "They are a Stiff-Necked People," *Christian Century* (August 30–September 6, 1989), 779.

4. Boff, *Church*, pp. 89, 92.

5. James B. Nelson, "Needed: A Continuing Sexual Revolution," *Christian Century* (June 1, 1988), 538-39.

6. Christina Larner, *Witchcraft and Religion: The Politics of Popular Belief* (New York: Basil Blackwell, 1984), pp. 99, 113.

7. Cited in Nelson, "Sexual Revolution," *Christian Century*, 540.

8. John Snow, *Mortal Fear* (Cambridge, MA: Cowley, 1987), p. 35.

9. Dozier, *Dream of God*, pp. 57-58.

10. Cited in Helene Cixous and Catherine Clement, *The Newly Born Woman*, trans. Betsy Wing (Minneapolis: University of Minnesota Press, 1986), p. 79; on the "double braid" of dualistic thought, see pp. 63-65.

11. Robert M. Cooper, "Intimacy," *St. Luke's Journal of Theology* Vol. 30 (March 1987), 116; Cooper focuses on intimacy expressing the *shalom* or peace of God.

12. May Sarton, *As We Are Now* (New York: W. W. Norton, 1973), p. 53.

13. Cited by Suzanne Gordon and Isabel Marcus in "Why We Need to Recover from Self-Fulfillment," *The Boston Sunday Globe* (June 24, 1990), A3.

14. A summary of research by James W. Prescott on violence and sexual pleasure noted in James B. Nelson, "Male Sexuality and Masculine Spirituality," *SIECUS Report*, Vol. 12, No. 4 (March 1985), 3-4.

15. John Welwood, *Journey of the Heart: Intimate Relationship and the Path of Love* (New York: Harper Perennial, 1990), p. 6.

16. Henri J. M. Nouwen, *Intimacy: Essays in Pastoral Psychology* (San Francisco: Harper & Row, 1969), p. 29.

17. Meeks, *God the Economist*, p. 11.

18. Boff, *Church*, p. 107.

19. John E. Booty, *What Makes Us Episcopalians?* (Wilton, CT: Morehouse-Barlow, 1982), p. 33.

20. *Theological Freedom and Social Responsibility*, Report of the Advisory Committee of the Episcopal Church, Stephen F. Bayne, Jr., Chairman (New York: The Seabury Press, 1967), p. 10.

owley Publications is a ministry of the Society of St. John the Evangelist, a religious community for men in the Episcopal Church. Emerging from the Society's tradition of prayer, theological reflection, and diversity of mission, the press is centered in the rich heritage of the Anglican Communion.

Cowley Publications seeks to provide books, audio cassettes, and other resources for the ongoing theological exploration and spiritual development of the Episcopal Church and others in the body of Christ. To this end, it is dedicated to developing a new generation of theological writers, encouraging them to produce timely, creative, and stimulating publications of excellence, and making these publications available widely, reaching both clergy and lay persons.